IMAGINATION FOR
A NEW GENERATION

North West England Vol III
Edited by Heather Killingray

Young Writers

First published in Great Britain in 2004 by:
Young Writers
Remus House
Coltsfoot Drive
Peterborough
PE2 9JX
Telephone: 01733 890066
Website: www.youngwriters.co.uk

All Rights Reserved

© *Copyright Contributors 2004*

SB ISBN 1 84460 633 3

Foreword

Young Writers was established in 1991 and has been passionately devoted to the promotion of reading and writing in children and young adults ever since. The quest continues today. Young Writers remains as committed to engendering the fostering of burgeoning poetic and literary talent as ever.

This year's Young Writers competition has proven as vibrant and dynamic as ever and we are delighted to present a showcase of the best poetry from across the UK. Each poem has been carefully selected from a wealth of *Once Upon A Rhyme* entries before ultimately being published in this, our twelfth primary school poetry series.

Once again, we have been supremely impressed by the overall high quality of the entries we have received. The imagination, energy and creativity which has gone into each young writer's entry made choosing the best poems a challenging and often difficult but ultimately hugely rewarding task - the general high standard of the work submitted amply vindicating this opportunity to bring their poetry to a larger appreciative audience.

We sincerely hope you are pleased with our final selection and that you will enjoy *Once Upon A Rhyme North West England Vol III* for many years to come.

Contents

Joseph Roberts (9)	1
Georgina Charnley (8)	1
Holly Whiston (10)	2
Zoe Lambrakis (11)	2

Beechwood Primary School
Philip Dean (11)	3
Liam Astley (11)	4

Booker Avenue Junior School
Jessica Murray (8)	4
Daniel Girling-Jones (9)	5
Hannah Crookall (9)	5

Childer Thornton Primary School
Thomas Coates (9)	5
Daniel Carolan (10)	6
Lewis Downes (11)	6
Luke O'Brien (11)	7
Katie Parr (10)	8

Constable Lee St Pauls CE Primary School
Coral Sunderland (10)	8
Shahzeb Mirza (9)	9

Devonshire Park Primary School
Katy Ginnetty (11)	10
Laura Swindlehurst (11)	10
Helen Downey (11)	11
Shaun Brown (11)	11
Megan Compton (11)	11
Kayleigh Pass (11)	12
Robin Wainwright (11)	12
Michelle Robson (11)	12
Megan Whalley (10)	13
Kate Ashcroft (11)	13

Jodie Robinson (11)	14
Liam Hayward (10)	14
Jennie Riley (11)	15
Daniel Hogan (11)	15
Christopher Turner (11)	16
Natalie Reynolds (10)	16
Katie McGrath (10)	17
Kyle Adams (11)	17
Abbie Billington (10)	18
Dominic John (11)	18
Sarah Gilbert (10)	19
Mary Barlow (10)	19

Eccleston Mere Primary School

Mark Brown (9)	19

Great Moor Junior School

Callum Bird (11)	20
Sophie Gilson (11)	20
Amy Bradbury (11)	21
Katie Sowter (11)	21
Jordan Evans (11)	22
Matthew Kenyon (11)	22
Joanna Steele (11)	23
Claudia Lewis (10)	23
Nadine Aly (10)	24

Holy Family School

Jordan Teebay (9)	24
Sammy Gillespie (10)	25
Jenny Lawson (10)	25
Sophie Barlow (10)	26
Samantha Calvert (10)	26
Joanne Stanley (10)	27
Karl Sivori-O'Neill (10)	27
Ross Bryan (10)	28
Joe Campbell (10)	28
Lois Kinvig (8)	29
Katherine Fairhurst (10)	29
Sophie Whittle (8)	29

Victoria Wignall (10)	30
Jennifer Culley (9)	30
Stephen Newton (9)	31
Jade Lambert (9)	31
Hannah Davison (9)	32
Daniel Lambert (11)	32
David Simpson (11)	33
Bethany Norris (8)	33
Conor Appleton (11)	34
Sophie Robinson (8)	34
John Brady (11)	35
Sophie O'Brien (7)	35
Helen O'Mara (11)	36
Daniel Krause (8)	36
Rebecca Chambers (10)	37
Rachael Bowen (8)	37
Rachel O'Toole (11)	38
Caitlin Wynn (10)	38
Max Thomas-McGenity (10)	39
Rosie O'Connor (11)	40
Conor Tiernan (10)	40
Ben Walker (11)	41
Rebecca Murphy (11)	41
Jessica Fogarty (7)	42
Glyn Wheeler (7)	42
Sophie Hilton (8)	42
Rebecca Wilkinson (11)	43
Emily Norris (10)	43
Daniel Dolan (11)	44
Robbie Sherman (8)	44
Rachel Howard (8)	44
Joseph Bennett (7)	45

Holy Spirit Catholic Primary School

Paul Sheridan (11)	45
Lauren Llewellyn (8)	46
Michael O'Brien (7)	46
Stevie Barton (8)	46
Alfie Lyon (11)	47
Nicole Burrows (8)	47
Natasha Harrison (8)	47

Hayden Morris (11)	48
Leoni Picton (8)	48
Gemma Coffey (11)	49
Shannon Duffy (8)	49
Chloe Lever (11)	50
Jon Tuffy (8)	50
Hannah Bamber (10)	51
Becky Bolton (11)	51
Heather Boland (11)	52

Howick CE Primary School

Gabrielle Critchley (10)	53
Yasir Mir (8)	53
Adam Barnish (8)	53
Emily Whalley (10)	54
Paris Maddock-Dickinson (9)	54

Kettleshulme St James' CE Primary School

Melissa Ross (9)	55
Harry Hill (7)	55
Dougal Mackenzie (9)	56
Anna Townley (7)	56
Lorenzo Llull-Grimshaw (8)	57
Lydia Royston (10)	57
Genna Carr (8)	58
Hollie Theloke (10)	58
Sophie Hopkin (11)	59
Daisy Tushaw (10)	59
Emma Booth (9)	60
Jenny Haselwood (11)	60
Megan Jackson (9)	61
Taylor McDonald-Webb (10)	61
Becky Lisle (8)	62

Kew Woods Primary School

Katie Whyte (10)	62
Jodie Altham (10)	63
Jessica Fletcher (9)	63
Aaron Lovelady (10)	64
Molly Bryson (10)	64

Jenny Craggs (11)	65
Christopher Benson (11)	65
Alex Couzens (9)	66
Mark McNorton (11)	66
Sophie Altham (8)	67
Kristian Roylance (11)	67
Abby Makin (8)	68
John Steel (11)	68
Jordan Crowney (10) & Philip Weston (11)	69
Lynn Koworera (10)	69
Kieran Rigby (8)	70
Jordan Sudlow-Lane (10)	70
Naomi Wilson (11)	71
Laura Eyes (10)	72
Jonathan Howard & Dean Orme (10)	72
Chloe Campbell (11)	73
Rebecca Jones (11)	73
Isabel Miranda N (11)	74
Siân Davies (9)	74
Victoria Hannah (10)	75
Daniel Lloyd (10)	75
Stuart Eyes & Meghan Standeven (11)	76
Amber Williams (11)	76
Jonathan Foster & Andrew Lea (11)	77
Lisa Jackson (10)	77
Rory Boyer (10) & Joseph Moran (11)	78
Katy Burgess-Cox (11)	78
Chowa Nkonde (10)	79
Billy Brookfield (9)	79
Ryan Burgess (10) & Curtis Rigby (11)	80
Chloe Fitton (10) & Mohammed Osman (11)	80
Jack Widdison & Amy Moore (11)	81
Daniel Lea (9)	81
Adam Monk (10) & Amro Mohamed (11)	82
Bobbie-Rose Warran (9)	82
Mathew Earle (8)	83
Stephen Roberts (11)	83
Sophie Wood (9)	84
Hannah Golland (9)	84
Jade Muncaster (8)	85
Connor Morris (9)	85
Jade Brothers (8)	86

Rebecca Moorhouse (9)	86
Sarah Murray (9)	87
Matthew Powell (8)	87
James Bailey (8)	88
Harry Standeven (9)	88
Bethany Clarke (9)	89
Michael James Casey (9)	89
Elise Bryson (10)	90

Kingsway Primary School

Anastasia Price (10)	90
Amal Ahmed (10)	91
Davie Dunlop (11)	92
Paul Lloyd (9)	92
Michael Davis (10)	93
Alexandra Lewis (10)	93
Jenna Griffiths (11)	94
Liam Gravett (10)	94
Jennie May (11)	95
Michael Wookey (11)	95
Ryan Bradley (11)	96
Matthew Bowie (11)	96
Kayleigh Pinch (11)	97
Jack Mercer (11)	97
Christopher Carson (11)	98
Jordan McWilliams (10)	98
Amelia Jenkins (10)	99
Sian Mason (10)	99
Liam Bradley (9)	100
Jake Parrott (10)	100
Lauren Randall (10)	100

Nether Kellett Community Primary School

Abbie Read (8)	101

North Cheshire Jewish Primary School

James Becker (9)	101
Jemma Becker (10)	102
Talya Lewis (9)	103

Our Lady's RC Primary School
    Emily Gandy (9) — 103

Our Lady's Catholic Primary School
    Rachael Galilee (11) — 104
    Leighton Anderson (10) — 104
    Connor Taylor (11) — 105
    Kimberley Darbyshire (11) — 105
    Adam Smith (11) — 105
    Alex Puddicombe (10) — 106
    Katie White (11) — 106
    CJ Anderson (9) — 107
    Beth Davies (11) — 107
    James McKeon (11) — 108
    Megan Duckworth (8) — 109
    Jake Brown (10) — 109
    Alex McKeon (9) — 110
    Jordan Rainford (11) — 110
    Ashleigh Kane (11) — 111
    Timothy McGuinness (10) — 111
    Michael Bradbury (9) — 112
    Natalie Gethins (8) — 112
    James Whibley (7) — 113
    Fern Baxter (10) — 113
    Nicole Rainford (9) — 114
    Liam Edwards (10) — 114
    Chloe McDermott (8) — 115
    Kate Livesey (8) — 115
    Nicholas Whibley (9) — 116
    Leah Hardman (8) — 117
    Andrew McDermott (10) — 117
    Antonia Swann (7) — 118
    Sadie McKeon (7) — 118
    Luke Verdon (11) — 118
    Olivia Ward (10) — 119
    Chase Anderson (7) — 119
    Nathan Stephenson (9) — 120
    Mathew Cameron (7) — 120
    Christien Galilee (10) — 121
    Sophie Rutter (8) — 121
    Charlotte McCann (8) — 122

Myles Dennett (9)	122
Emma Titcombe (9)	123
Callum Wright (9)	123
Charlotte Williams (9)	124
Jordan Kane (9)	124
Niall Winn (8)	125
Rebecca Delooze (9)	125

Penketh Community Primary School

Matthew Twiss (11)	126
Christopher Venables (10)	126
Samantha Craven (11)	127
Rachel Brownbill (11)	127
Amie Smith (11)	128
Emily Hedgcock (11)	128
Adam Rowles (11)	129
Samantha Worrall (11)	129
Emily Stockton (10)	130
Sophie Gamon (10)	130
Philippa Wheatley (11)	131
Leanne Graham (11)	131
Jack Karran (11)	132
Alex Evans (11)	133
Melissa Doan (11)	134
Rebecca Casey (10)	135
Lucy Beech (11)	136
Alec Walker (11)	137
Jessica McDonald (11)	138

Poulton Lancelyn Primary School

Frank Richards (9)	138
Bethany Gerrard (7)	139
Laura O'Meara (11)	139
James McIver (9)	140
Katie Hastings (9)	140
Laura Armand (11)	140
Lorna Hayden (8)	141
Dulcie Wilkinson (9)	141
Emma Maddocks (11)	142
Ruth Buddle (9)	142
Scott Richardson (9)	143

Lewis Evans (11)	143
Melissa Noble (8)	143
Aaron Smith (10)	144
Natalie Carpenter (9)	144
Emilie Sutcliffe (9)	145
Matthew Dobson (9)	145
Natalie Fields (9)	146
Fern Gordon (10)	146
Abigail Elias (9)	147
Katie McIver (9)	147
Jamie Morris (8)	147
Abhijith Thippeswamy (11)	148
Zoë Brunton (9)	148
Joe Cullen (10)	149
Lauren Price (10)	149
Louise Jones (8)	150
Molly Dyas (10)	150
Rachel Winstanley (9)	150

Queens Road Primary School

Matthew Hicks (7)	151

St Margaret Mary's Junior School, Liverpool

Gabrielle Flude (7)	151

St Mary's CE Primary School, Wirral

Lewis Joinson (9)	151
Amy Edwards (9)	152
Eleanor Caitlin Chambers (9)	152
Kelsie Oldfield (8)	152
Tom Davies (8)	153
Heather Hillbeck (8)	153
Sarah Edwards (7)	153
William Foster (8)	154
Connor Barry (9)	154
Conor Hallwood (7)	154
Daniel Reece (7)	155
Jessica Nevitt (8)	155

St Pauls RC Primary School, Blackburn
Charlotte Smith (9) — 155
Jade Duxbury (8) — 156
Charlotte Hindle (9) — 156
Nicole Cassidy (9) — 156
Katrina Tomlinson (8) — 157

St Teresa's RC Primary School, Irlam
Ben Hanley (7) — 157
Joseph Denneny (7) — 157
Alex Lightfoot (7) — 158
Lewis Holland (7) — 158
Christopher Davenport (7) — 159
Georgia Burbidge (7) — 159
Kieran Farrell (7) — 159
Alex Nelson (7) — 160

St Peter's CE Primary School, Wirral
Lewis Horrocks (11) & Polly Pattinson (10) — 160
Bethany Gillen (9) — 161
Nicholas Jones (9) — 161
Edward Gibbs (10) — 162
Katherine Astbury (7) — 162
Emily Yates (9) — 163
Harry Twells (10) — 163
Jessica Rushworth (9) — 164
Natalie Lowry (9) — 164
Alasdair Cunningham (10) — 165
Lily Taylor (11) — 165
Alistair Jones (11) — 166
Ben Robinson (10) — 166
Joe Clarke (9) — 167
Elle Lawrenson (11) — 167
Sophie Kellner (9) — 168
Zoe Turner (10) — 168
Hannah Dowler (10) — 169
Claire Murray (10) — 169
Aidan Mould (8) — 170
Amanda Trenholm & Zoe Williamson (11) — 170
Laura Dawson & Sarah Rothwell (11) — 171

Kate Hill (11)	171
Natasha Doyle (11)	172
Alex Hazlehurst (9)	172
Josh Beck (11)	173
Nicole Page (9)	173
Amy Williams (11)	174
Emily Clarke (9)	174
Sarah Browning (10)	175
Rebecca Leeman (9)	175
Lucy Roberts (9)	176
Elizabeth Williamson (9)	176
Hannah Rowlands (11)	177
Rachel Cooke (10) & Bethany Da Forno (9)	178
Lilley Orme (10)	178

SS Peter & Paul RC Primary School

Anthony Brear (11)	178
Georgina Edwards (11)	179
Alex Howard (11)	179
Nicole Haviland (11)	180
Sarah Hoyle (10)	180
Thomas Moscrip (10)	181
Tom McHugh (11)	181
Kathryn Poyning (10)	182
Alex Sawyer (11)	182
Ashley Breckell (10)	183
Amy Jones (10)	183
Charlotte Edwards (10)	184
Katie Menear (11)	184
Rebecca McGarry (10)	185
Kate Burnett (11)	185
Benedict Gillett (10)	185
Hannah Heathcote (11)	186
Jazz Adams (11)	186
Rosie Cull (10)	186
Josh Rylance (10)	187
Maria Noone (9)	187
Shay Donnelly (10)	188
Callum Hibbard (10)	188
Lucinda Crosby (10)	189
Daine Boden (10)	189

Charles Nethercoat (9) — 189
Bethany Cumming (10) — 190
Elliott McWilliam (10) — 190

Woodley Primary School
Darcey Moores (9) — 191
Ellie Worsley (9) — 191
Lewis Moore & Daniel Allen-Prince (9) — 191
Amy Redfearn (9) — 192
Ben McKinstry (9) — 192
Lydia Boswell (8) — 192
Joe Brennan (9) — 193
Jessica Martin (9) — 193
Toby Leigh (9) — 193
Natalie Davies (9) — 194
Leah Brown (9) — 194
Alesha Cresswell (9) — 194
Rachael Thomas (9) — 195
Ashley Dearden (9) — 195
Rachael Millward (9) — 195
Sophie Drummond (9) — 196
Kimberley Robinson (9) — 196
Lewis Curbishley (9) — 196
Ben Annable (7) — 197
Rebecca Cashin (8) — 197
Jake McCormack (8) — 197
Billy Gaskell (7) — 198
Nicholas Moorby (8) — 198
Hannah Cooper (10) — 198
Megan Ormiston (7) — 199
Michael Turner (8) — 199
Olivia Wild (7) — 199
Thomas Hart (7) — 200
Emily Stanyer (7) — 200
Grace Wootton (8) — 200
Matthew Day (9) — 201
Katie Fowler (9) — 201
Jessica Barlow (9) — 202
Nicole Clarke (8) — 202
Rhianna Scott (8) — 202
Alyson Lees (9) — 203

Peter Harrop (9)   203
Kristina Rudge (8)   203
Robert Fox (9)   203
Hannah Stevens (9)   204

The Poems

The Time Capsule

Stainless steel, black inside,
The time capsule, silent, hides
Dairy milk, a rubber band,
A pencil and a cola can,
A spider runs across the rim,
The time capsule, now put in,
Dark and lonely underground,
The time capsule, to be found.

Underneath the ground it lies,
Unseen to future people's eyes,
An oak tree root curls around,
The time capsule, tightly bound.
Cutting through the root, a spade,
Uncovers the time capsule, gently laid,
Dirty, battered, cased in glass,
The time capsule, found at last.

Joseph Roberts (9)

The Farm

There was an old animal farm
It was so deadly calm
You could not hear a cow
Or the brum from a plough
And then I heard an alarm.

One day a man came to visit
I was naming a lamb 'Wizzit'
The pig said, 'Hello'
From deep down below
And the horse said, 'My name is Fizzit!'

Georgina Charnley (8)

On Opening A Book . . .

When you open a book,
You smell a smell
Of excitement in a world
Of fresh pages.

When you open a book,
You hear voices
Whispering a brand new story
In your mind.

When you open a book
You feel a feeling
Of suspense and wonder
From words that tingle.

When you close a book
It's annoying!

Holly Whiston (10)

The Cold

A tall white man laying his stare on you,
His sad glum face looks out far into unknown places.
He comes to your house to lay his icy breath on your doorstep.
The cold.
An animal that growls at you,
Tugs at your clothes and bites at your flesh.
The cold.
His brother is the fog, his sister is the rain.
His father is the storm that lumbers through the sky.
The cold.
One day the warmer weather will come.
Both man and animal will leave to haunt some other house.
But till then they must walk their icy path.
The cold.

Zoe Lambrakis (11)

Nature's Wonders

Murky water shimmers and splashes,
As children clumsily waft about with their nets,
Weeds are elaborate,
Conquering the pond they provide a sanctuary for the wildlife,
Outcasts on the edge of the green crowd throb with no support,
The decking supports playful children with stained sturdy planks,
Overshadowing, it hugs and gradually conquers the pond's surface.
A sluggish tree comes to a standstill,
Embedding its foundations into the soil.
Now it towers aloft reaching for the sky,
Stretching its huge arms out casting a shadow,
It intimidates the inferior undergrowth,
But a silent stalker waits.
It stalks the giant tree circling until it has a grip,
Then reaching its coils high, creeps up the trunk,
Once there it becomes jealous of the trees superior strength,
So plans to conquer, tightens its grip,
Soon the once dull, brown bank is taken over by a green carpet,
The ivy tries to strangle and smother but fails,
So continues to scale the mighty beast.
Jagged rocks expand across the shore,
Supporting seed cases in grooves and crevasses,
While smooth pebbles huddle together,
Hiding in the shadow of larger rocks,
Wind steals twigs and feeble leaves from their homes,
The air is salty, reminding me of illness.
The world a kaleidoscope of colours and settings,
Dull to sparkling,
Shadowy corners into overflowing sunset sky,
Nature continues to mystify men forever.

Philip Dean (11)
Beechwood Primary School

Captivating Conway And Magical Menai

Creatures skimming across the murky pond surface energetically,
Escaping the threat of nets randomly splashing into their home of disturbed weeds.
The dull surface reflects the dim sky,
Shadows lurk, waiting.

Woodland, shadowed by the towering trees, ivy covering and rising,
A lilac haze of bluebells in the distance where the sun shines brightly.
The birds' high pitched songs, echoing to their hidden friends,
Rustling leaves crunch beneath.

Incredible views of overlappping mountains in a contest to reach the faraway sun,
Eventually collide with the gentle, clear sky.
The jet soars with its deafening engines,
Whilst the birds chirp their unique tunes, joyfully.

The sparkling sea glistens and with the tide on his side, prevents humans from reaching his secret beaches,
Seaweed hangs like coats from the rock.
The drum-like sounds of two canoes banging together double like a heartbeat.
Slippery rocks are trap doors.

Liam Astley (11)
Beechwood Primary School

In The Winter

In the winter the trees are bare,
With all the leaves on the ground,
Sun hiding behind the clouds,
The wind is cold,
The nights are dark,
Moon is shining up alone,
Stars are twinkling in the dark night sky,
Next is spring where the flowers are blossoming,
The sun is rising, bright and warm.

Jessica Murray (8)
Booker Avenue Junior School

Winter Is

Winter is when there's no leaves on the trees
Winter is when drops of snow land on the pavement
Winter is when Christmas arrives
Winter is when rain hits people's heads
Winter is when you buy a Christmas tree
Winter is my favourite season.

Daniel Girling-Jones (9)
Booker Avenue Junior School

Animals!

As tall as a giraffe's neck reaching up to the leaves
As small as a monkey swinging from tree to tree
As soft as a rabbit asleep under a tree trembling with fear
As fierce as a lion pouncing at its prey.

Hannah Crookall (9)
Booker Avenue Junior School

The Magic Door

Once there was an old oak door
With black bolts like pebbles of stone
And in the door there was nothing in reality
But something in you
Something magical, something special
When you walk through
You will find what you have always wanted
And you cannot break the door with a hammer
Nor any other tool you may find
But you can ruin it by wanting revenge
And one day I walked into that room
Where the door was
But found it had gone.

Thomas Coates (9)
Childer Thornton Primary School

The Window

You can beam through the window
But don't scream through the window

You can crawl through the window
But don't fall through the window

You can peek through the window
But don't give cheek through the window

You can eat peach through the window
But don't screech through the window

You can gaze through the window
But don't laze through the window

You can cry through the window
But don't fly through the window.

Daniel Carolan (10)
Childer Thornton Primary School

Door Chorus

While the old oak front door bangs proudly
The new swinging kitchen door squeaks
With a friendly tone.

Meanwhile, the middle-aged pine door clicks gently
But that rusted ancient cellar door groans
Threateningly.

The ignored smooth attic door snaps angrily
But not before the sanded lounge door
Goes to assuringly

The airing cupboard door creaks gently

But my bedroom door shuts without a sound
Fortunately!

Lewis Downes (11)
Childer Thornton Primary School

Through That Door

Through that door
Over there
There's nothing to do
But sit and stare

If you watch
The night
Then morning
Comes light

Day passes by
Look
Planes fly
And birds try
To glide
The wind

Herds of elephant
Pound the ground
Trample grass down
Down

Through that door
There's a park
Catch it! Catch it!
Here comes the dark.

Luke O'Brien (11)
Childer Thornton Primary School

The Door's Voice

Each door has a different voice

The old oak door to the castle
Has a loud and scary slam

Whilst the painted door to the attic
Makes a soft and whispery click

Each door has a different voice

The arched door to the house
Squeaks and needs oiling

However, the fire door in school
Is silent until it hits the wall

Each door has a different voice

The large door that opens Hartington Hall
Has a deafening and threatening voice

But the door of the tiny doll's house
Is so shy, it's inaudible.

Katie Parr (10)
Childer Thornton Primary School

Coral And Family

My dad is mad
My mum is glum
My sister has a big blister
My dog ate a fat frog
My guinea pig wears a bushy wig
My fish hope and wish
And me, I live under the sea.

Coral Sunderland (10)
Constable Lee St Pauls CE Primary School

My Pet Mouse!

My pet
Is
Furry

My pet's
Got
A tail

My pet
Doesn't
Fly
Or sing

But
My pet's
A cute
Thing.

But
My pet
Lives In
A house.

For
My pet
Is a

Squeaky
Freaky
Beauty
Suited
Small
And
Furry . . .
Mouse!

Shahzeb Mirza (9)
Constable Lee St Pauls CE Primary School

What's In The Teacher's Cupboard?

It could be grimy,
It could be slimy,
There could be ants from France,
Or spiders that dance.
There could be mouldy sweets
Or the hardest maths sheets
What's in the teacher's cupboard?

There could be old beef
Oh, good grief,
There could be the teacher's slippers
Or even fish flippers.
There could be broken glass,
Or last year's class,
Oh, what's in the teacher's cupboard?

There could be people she's hated,
Or even people she's dated.
There could be 1997's Yellow Pages,
That no one's seen in ages,
What's in the teacher's cupboard?

Katy Ginnetty (11)
Devonshire Park Primary School

My Family

My nan's gone off her head,
My grandad's surely dead,
Mum loves to jive,
My sixteen year old brother acts like he's five,
My dad likes to collect conkers,
While my sister's gone bonkers,
My auntie is always in Spain,
And my uncle's just a pain,
One of my cousins wears big pants,
My other one lives in France,
And there's me, I'm just normal.

Laura Swindlehurst (11)
Devonshire Park Primary School

Nature

Trees and plants wild in their bloom,
Pretty blue flowers searching for room,
Butterflies and bees flying away,
Pollen from flowers which will be taken some day.

For metres they spread, ages and more,
Moments together while bugs all crawl,
Make the fields feel free and fresh
While being inside the countryside's flesh.

Helen Downey (11)
Devonshire Park Primary School

Football

F ootball is the best sport ever
O n the day Gerrard scored a hat-trick
O f course you don't know when the game's unfurled
T ook the ball and scored all again
B alls are shooting at the goal by Liverpool
A ll the games Liverpool have won are amazing
L ook at all the games they've played
L iverpool always win the league.

Shaun Brown (11)
Devonshire Park Primary School

Dolphins

D olphins are cool
O ver they go
L eaping over the sea,
P laying around with all of their friends
H aving fun all the time
I n a fight with a shark they can win in a flash
N othing will scare them not even a whale
S ome are in danger so take care of them please.

Megan Compton (11)
Devonshire Park Primary School

The Girl Who Loves The Sea

When she goes to the sea
She sits on her mum's knee,
Watching the boats go by,
Oh, it makes her cry,
The salty smell in the air,
She feels like there's no care in the world.
Seagulls flying all around
And people digging in the ground.
She goes home with her mum,
Oh, she loves to go to the sea,
Sitting on her mum's knee.

Kayleigh Pass (11)
Devonshire Park Primary School

Piranha!

I saw a man fall in the Amazon,
'Please help me, please do!' said he.
'I'm sorry,' I said, 'but if I jumped in,
The piranha would relish me!'

'What piranha?' he asked, looking around,
His eyes wide with terrible fright.
They attacked him, poor man and then I spoke:
'Good Heavens, Sir! Are you alright?'

Robin Wainwright (11)
Devonshire Park Primary School

School

S tanding in the playground with all my friends
C lasses of children working hard
H eads on tables
O ur class sitting down
O n goes the overhead projector
L istening to the teacher.

Michelle Robson (11)
Devonshire Park Primary School

My Funny Family

First there's my mum now that's a long story,
She climbed on a roof and ran off with Rory.

Then there's my dad he always calls you lad,
Everybody thinks he's mad because he's my dad.

Then there's my sister she went on the twister
And got an enormous blister.

James is my brother,
Who once thought he was my mother.

My dog is called Molly,
She once ate her dolly called Polly.

My nan is so old,
She looks like a piece of mould.

But I'm so glad because they're my family.

Megan Whalley (10)
Devonshire Park Primary School

A Storm

I can flash my torch in the middle of the night,
When I play my drum I give children a fright,
When I am annoyed I can pick up houses
And move seas,
I can make the leaves come off the old willow trees.

When I come out all the children go in,
I can knock things over such as the bin,
I can make things swirl in the sky,
When I howl and scream, babies cry.

When I sit alone the sky goes black and grey in sorrow,
Now all the adults wonder what will happen tomorrow.

Kate Ashcroft (11)
Devonshire Park Primary School

Monster!

There's something in my sister's room,
It's ugly and it's green,
The monster is smelly but really clean,
It always pulls my covers off me in the night,
This nasty monster has given me a really bad fright,
It has eaten all my toys,
And it really hates noise,
It's coming down the landing,
It's coming closer to my door,
I see the door start to slide open,
I run towards it,
The door slides fully open
I jump in front of my door,
The monster runs back into my sister's room,
And I don't think it will be back anymore.

Jodie Robinson (11)
Devonshire Park Primary School

Have A Lullaby

Relax all day
But you'll have to pay
Don't say you don't want to,
If you say yes, you'll feel new.

Massage, a wax, and a feet rub,
You'll relax all day in a bathtub,
At the end you'll feel beautiful
And of course it is suitable.

It only lasts one hour
At the beginning you'll feel like flower,
Halfway through you'll feel light
At the end you'll say it was worth it.

Liam Hayward (10)
Devonshire Park Primary School

My Mum

My mum is such a pain
I feel like flushing her down the drain
I get really annoyed when she calls me hun,
But sometimes she can be really fun.

I think my mum is really looney,
Because she wants to meet George Clooney.
When I try to put on her shoes,
She always knows because I leave clues.

My mum is so amazing,
Although I wonder why she's lazing,
I can't believe I'm related to her,
Now that's something I can never bear.

I think my mum is really kind,
She was the best that I could find.
I think my mum is really pretty,
She looks like my lovely kitty.

Jennie Riley (11)
Devonshire Park Primary School

Thierry Henry

Henry, Henry, the hat trick hero
Henry, Henry, the score was 4-3
Such talent, such skill for all to see
Henry, Henry, the man of the match for
Arsenal he is such a catch
When he gets the ball he makes it dance
Henry, Henry, our man from France.

When Highbury's supporters one and all
Shout, 'Come on ref, that's Henry's ball'
And when the Gunners are in the bootroom
They all stamp their feet and shout
    Va Va Voom!

Daniel Hogan (11)
Devonshire Park Primary School

There's A Monster Under The Bed

There's a monster under the bed,
With horrid yellow eyes,
There's a monster under the bed,
Who scares you by surprise,
There's a monster under the bed,
Who has smelly, slimy feet,
There's a monster under the bed,
Which likes to eat meat,
There's a monster under the bed,
With horrid scaly skin,
There's a monster under the bed,
Which sometimes eats out of my bin,
There's a monster under the bed,
Who is very, very scary,
There's a monster under the bed,
Who can fight off any fairy,
There's a monster under the bed,
Who's very, very smelly,
There's a monster under the bed,
Which ate my old welly,
There's a monster under the bed,
So I went and told my mother,
There's a monster under the bed,
Which turned out to be my brother.

Christopher Turner (11)
Devonshire Park Primary School

My Friends

Katie Holmes loves to sing
Cara Wilson is a performer
Samantha is a slow learner
Leanne is loud in the dance hall
Bethan loves going bowling
And there's me and my best friend Megan
And we are totally addicted to fun.

Natalie Reynolds (10)
Devonshire Park Primary School

Surprise

I am eleven today
Yes it is my birthday
I am having a party but I don't know when,
Mum baking me a cake
But why? I am not having my party now,
Who are those presents?
Mum telling me to go upstairs
But why?
The doorbell's ringing,
The door's opening and closing all the time,
Dad said, 'I have a surprise for you,'
But why?
My hands are shaking
My eyes are closed ready to open,
Dad opens the door,
Everybody said *surprise!*
I am glad I had my party today.

Katie McGrath (10)
Devonshire Park Primary School

Supermarkets

If there wasn't any supermarkets
There wouldn't be any fun,
There would be no place to run down aisles
As fast as a speeding bullet.
If there wasn't any
Supermarkets there wouldn't be any fun,
There would be no place to skid along on
The trolleys or have races to the checkouts.
There would be no place to plead your
Mum to buy you the newest computer game.
There would be no place to scream or shout
If there wasn't any supermarkets!

Kyle Adams (11)
Devonshire Park Primary School

My Family

There is my mum
She calls me hun
But she is a lot of fun.

Then there's my dad
Who is totally mad
But makes me happy when I am sad.

There is this boy
Who is my brother,
I couldn't change him
For another.

Then there is me
Who is a regular girl,
And who loves her family
In the whole wide world.

Abbie Billington (10)
Devonshire Park Primary School

Bodybuilding

B ulging biceps are very big
O rgan orange juice
D rinking quickly
Y ummy
B eautiful press ups
U p to forty
I n the gym
L ooking healthy
D renched in sweat
I nto the shower
N ow he's clean
G igantic genetics.

Dominic John (11)
Devonshire Park Primary School

Flowers

The flowers stand still
Grows in the watery soil
Grows in the sunlight.

Stem is falling down
All the petals falling down
Flowers falling down.

Sarah Gilbert (10)
Devonshire Park Primary School

Flowers

Beautiful flower
Morning comes, flowers awake
Flowers beg for water.

Petals fall softly
Autumn is coming quietly
Life is now beginning.

Mary Barlow (10)
Devonshire Park Primary School

The Mental Mega Dog

I am the mentalest dog in the world
I don't eat dog food
I wolf down fairy dust
I don't drink water or milk
I suck the Earth's gravity and gulp the sky
I don't sleep on a bed
I doze off in a cloud of dinky dwarves
I don't chase cats or cars
I speed after shooting stars and atomic asteroids
I fly in space like no other dog could
I don't need a space helmet
I am mental mega dog.

Mark Brown (9)
Eccleston Mere Primary School

In The Air Raid Shelters

I could smell mould on the walls
I could smell sand in the air
I could smell sick on the beds
I could smell death everywhere

I could hear the whistling bombs
I could hear the shrieking planes
I could hear the crackling flames
I could hear death everywhere

I could see the beds full of horrified people
I could see the floor covered in dirty water
I could see the blood on the walls
I could see death everywhere.

I could feel the freezing walls shudder
I could feel the people's tears
I could feel the blackness stabbing me,
I could feel death everywhere.

Callum Bird (11)
Great Moor Junior School

In The Air Raid

I was alone
It was cold
It was dark
Big and bold
Secrets being told.
I can hear people in fear,
They are coming closer and near
I can feel tears coming down my cheek
I want this war to end this week
I am cold
And the dark is big and bold
I just want my family
To hold me.

Sophie Gilson (11)
Great Moor Junior School

Tunnels And Tubes . . .

T unnels, tunnels when will they stop?
U nder the ground, under the rock,
N urse Twig has got the mop
N o one's there, should I knock?
E veryone's gone it's all very silent
L ots of bombs are being dropped they're so violent.

A fter that we are allowed out
N ow that's the all clear
D oubtful I wander about

T here's people around, they're full of beer,
U nder the ground we have to go again
B ut this time it's worse
E veryone's here and they are going to remain
S o tonight will be a very long night!

Amy Bradbury (11)
Great Moor Junior School

Awful Air Raid Shelters

It was really dark and cold down there
Full of damp and smelly air
Lots of people cramped up tight
Lots of people quivering with fright
People singing to keep them happy
The toilets smell of a used nappy
Well me, I was cramped up tight
Trying to smile with all my might
A tear rolled down my gloomy face,
I stood up and walked at a very slow pace.
Then I heard the all clear bell,
Hooray, I was out of this horrible cell.
I was out! The sunlight was blinding
But . . . but . . . my home was destroyed, I was homeless.

Katie Sowter (11)
Great Moor Junior School

Shelters

Lay on my top bunk
I thought of my family,
The noises were giving me a headache
People singing, shouting, talking,
Bombs exploding sirens roaring!

It was cold
My blankets were wet
I was nervous, upset,
I could hardly open my eyes
The sandstone was crumbling
It was falling in my eyes!

Before I knew it, my host mother was shaking me
'Wake up, sleepy head!' she shouted.
'The all clear siren is going!'
I got up
The shelters were deserted
They were silent.

Jordan Evans (11)
Great Moor Junior School

Hitler Will Go Down

I hate that Hitler he took me from my family
I hate those German planes they blew up my home
I hate those German men they should not have
Taken Poland.

I love those shelters they saved me from a bomb,
I love the England men they will make us win the war.
I love our planes they will bomb Germany
We will bomb the men so they will not come again
Hitler has gone down so we will wear the crown.

Matthew Kenyon (11)
Great Moor Junior School

They're Here!

A ny time they can come, any place
I ce cold underneath
R aining rapidly, lightning too

R aids begin, they're here, what should I do?
A ction begins
I 'm frightened, squashed too, I want my mum
D arkness above us, it's the blackout

S ongs begin to cheer us up
H itler will pay for what he does all day
E veryone's joyful
L aughter begins . . .
T he bombs *bang! crash!* Stop
E veryone's gone, fire everywhere up there
R ain has begun!

Joanna Steele (11)
Great Moor Junior School

In The Shelters

I was nervous
I was scared
The wardens helped
And really cared.
Children were crying
Grown ups too
I was frightened
You would be too
The shelters were damp and cold
Some people young
Some people old
In the shelters underground
People talked
And wandered round.

Claudia Lewis (10)
Great Moor Junior School

Air Raid Shelters . . .

What's that noise?
What's that!
Unsure,
Frightened,
Worried,
Scared,
That's how I feel now
Not like it used to be
Everything's different
And everyone's different
It's not the same
I used to like the fame
Excited,
Jolly,
Happy,
Distinctive,
I'm feeling happy as
We come out of the shelter
Everything starting to
Come together!

    Evacuee . . .
    Evacuee . . .

Nadine Aly (10)
Great Moor Junior School

Food

Food yummy food
We cannot do without it
Is there anything better than beans on toast?
I seriously doubt!

Jordan Teebay (9)
Holy Family School

Horrible Homework Perfect Poetry

I hate homework it drives me mad
Doing it makes me feel sad
Please someone do it for me now
In comes Mum to have a row
My mum says it's good for me
When all she does is sits and drinks tea.

I hate reading it's no fun
I'd rather be shot by a firing gun
My mum makes me read every night
If I don't she puts up a fight.

I hate spelling so very much
To me it looks like double dutch
My mum says practise all the time
In the spelling test you'll do fine.

I hate maths lots and lots
More than I hate having spots
My mum never makes any sense
I think my brain's jumped over a fence.

I love poetry it's really, really cool
I love the way it rhymes, we do it in school
My mum thinks I'm a really good poet
I'm good at rhymes and I know it.
I'm really not telling any lies
I know that I could win this . . . award.

Sammy Gillespie (10)
Holy Family School

Poem

A short rhyming song
Which is sometimes very long
It nearly always rhymes
At lots of different times.

Jenny Lawson (10)
Holy Family School

My Uncle Ronnie

My uncle Ronnie has two kids
And two enormous feet.
He has a wife called Karen
He always keeps things nice and neat.

My uncle Ronnie cleans the house
And makes us clean the car
It has to be so perfect he's very la-de-dar.

And when he does the garden
Everybody knows he cuts the grass
With scissors and puts the worms in rows.

So if you want to meet him
I'll say the answer's yes
But whatever you do
Don't make a mess.

Sophie Barlow (10)
Holy Family School

Belt Up In The Back!

Are we nearly there yet?
Can I have a sweet?
Are we nearly there yet?
Quick, I need the toilet!

Are we nearly there yet?
Will you read me a story?
Are we nearly there yet?
Quick, I need the toilet!

Are we nearly there yet?
I need something to eat!
Are we nearly there yet?
Quick I'm going to wet
    Myself!

Samantha Calvert (10)
Holy Family School

Poem Competitions

P oem competitions really rule
O n the day it will be really cool
E very day I set my mind
M any rhymes I will find.

C ome along and hear the cheer
O h Dad stop drinking beer
M other Mary make me win
P lease Lord then I won't sin
E verything's going great now
T he family they all said wow
I am as nervous as can be
T oday's the day that I will see
I f I win or if I lose
O ur whole family will be drinking booze
N ow my friend Hannah
S till cheers me on with the Copacabana.

Joanne Stanley (10)
Holy Family School

Who Invented School

Who invented school?
It's really, really cool
I learn a lot of stuff
I'm really, really chuffed
I arrive at school with a smile
And chat to my friends for a while
We play out at half past ten
We'll probably play tag again
Are we on the grass today?
The sun is out today and we all shout, 'Hooray!'

Karl Sivori-O'Neill (10)
Holy Family School

The Match

We came out of the tunnel
With confidence and hope
As soon as we kicked off
We thought we couldn't cope.

They had the ball all the time
Eventually the ball was mine.

The manager gave me a bit of luck
I ended up in a sludge of muck.

The people were shouting *'Pass the ball'*
The people I passed to were ever so small.

He got the ball he lost the ball
But then they were on the attack.

I couldn't bear to watch then . . .
Suddenly I heard a *whack!* . . . Goal.

Ross Bryan (10)
Holy Family School

Rugby World Cup

R olls Royces
U nder pressure
G reat clothes
B ig fans
Y ears of work

W onderful time
O *ff!* says the ref
R ed cards
L ots of money
D ancing the Haka

C up winners
U gly faces
P lay this game forever.

Joe Campbell (10)
Holy Family School

The Sea Makes Me Think Of . . .

The fish running round my knee
Like a buzzing bee.

The dolphins leap high in the air
As I fall on my sun chair
Falling fast asleep.

The waves reach the shore
As they chase my toes
As I splish and splash in the waves.

Lois Kinvig (8)
Holy Family School

Queen Victoria Kenning

Long liver,
Throne keeper,
Bad mother,
Husband lover,
Great ruler,
Empire reigner,
Black wearer,
Nation carer.

Katherine Fairhurst (10)
Holy Family School

The Sea

When I go to the sea
You can come with me.
We will jump in the sea waves
And find hidden treasure in
Underground caves.
When the waves come
I will eat a plum.

Sophie Whittle (8)
Holy Family School

Poem Competition

P oem competitions are so cool
O nly because they rule.
E veryone loves them and I do too
M y friend won one, her name is Sue.

C ompany while I write them
O h help me please dear pen
M y poems are so great
P lenty of help from my mate
E very day I write a line
T oday I have written nine
I f my mind turns all blank
T eacher helps me, many thanks
I think I'm finished now
O h please can I take a bow?
N o please don't make me write any more
S leepy, sleepy eyes and hands so sore.

Victoria Wignall (10)
Holy Family School

Our School

We have the best school
It's better than having a swimming pool.

All the teachers are so funny
They are cute as a bunny.

Mrs McConnell's hair is so short
She is really good at sports.

We have a helper in our class
She sometimes takes us to Mass.

Jennifer Culley (9)
Holy Family School

My Head's Missing

My head's missing, it's been gone all day
My head is missing and my brother said Hooray.

I know it may sound stupid about my head
But the boy who kicked it off was called Fred.

He kicked the ball in a blast that's the plot
Next thing you know it was off with a shot.

Now I don't have any vision for now or never
And I can't see danger it comes whenever.

It's not fair I cannot see a thing
But now Mum's glad because I cannot sing.

It's really, really not fair I cannot do a thing
But what will this headless adventure ever bring?

Stephen Newton (9)
Holy Family School

School Toilet Blues

Monday's child
Is on the loo
Tuesday's child
Needs it too
Wednesday's child
Blows her nose
Thursday's child
Looks in the mirror to pose
Friday's child
Gets paper towels
Saturday's child
Has funny bowels
But the child born on the Sabbath day
Went before they came to school.

Jade Lambert (9)
Holy Family School

The Trouble With Teachers

The teachers in my school
Are really, really cool.
They put a lot of thought
Into my school report.
They let us play out
And never even shout,
But . . .

Miss Plump has the biggest bum and can't fit
Through the door
And old Miss Wicket is mad about cricket
And goes on for evermore.
Mrs Witch has a black cat and really freaks me out
And Mrs Pig is really big and her nose looks like a snout.

But my teacher has a lovely face (I better put that just in case!)
She is so pretty she earns her pay
I wouldn't swap her any day.

Hannah Davison (9)
Holy Family School

Football

Football it's a beautiful game
Anyone who hates it is pretty lame
Liverpool it's my favourite team
Every piece of clothing they wear,
It seems to gleam.

Everton one of the worst teams in football
Every time they get the ball they always trip and fall.
Everytime footballers get mad the ball gets hurled
Because football is the best game in the world.

Daniel Lambert (11)
Holy Family School

The Sky Of Storms

The sky can be very cloudy
The sky can also be clear
The sky can cheer up everyone
Each and every year.

The clouds can make up characters
From cartoons to books
But it's really up to you
Of how the clouds look.

Aeroplanes glide across
Helicopters hover high
Gliders soar in
The fantastic sapphire sky.

The midnight hurricane
It's made its way into town
Only the sky is safe because
It's high up off the ground.

The dawn of the sky
Smells of summer bloom
But the human race
Has met its doom.

Tornadoes strong,
Twisters of power
This may be our last month,
Day or hour . . .

David Simpson (11)
Holy Family School

A Sunny Day

Sunny days make me bright
My head feels light and fuzzy.
It makes me wink and blink
And squint
And makes my limbs very heavy.

Bethany Norris (8)
Holy Family School

The Deep Blue Dramatic Sea

The deep blue dramatic sea
Goes down, down, down
The deep blue sparkling sea
Shining like a golden crown.

The deep blue lively sea
Has lots of weird things
The deep blue dancing sea
Always has time to sing.

The deep blue flowing sea
Moving in the breeze
The deep blue forceful sea
Ignoring sailors pleas.

The deep blue shining sea
Sparkling in the sun
The deep blue amazing sea
Always having fun.

The deep blue fantastical sea
With a home for lots of fish
The deep blue exciting sea
Really is quite blue.

The deep blue excellent sea
Sparkling in the sun
The sea seems like it's coming to an end
When it's really just begun!

Conor Appleton (11)
Holy Family School

Sunny Day

On a sunny day
When the girls come out to play
Everyone sings and says hooray!
I play and play until the sun goes away
I look forward to seeing it another day!

Sophie Robinson (8)
Holy Family School

Hypedd

Many travellers have seeked out the land
But many have disappeared and are dead
They are lucky for no one has escaped from
The land of *Hypedd*.

Some people say it is the Hell
In deep terrible red
For no one has returned from
The Land of *Hypedd*.

The ones who have survived
Are living but also dead
For they have been terribly cursed
By the land of *Hypedd*.

Tales have been told
And people have had visions in bed
Of the perilous, spine-chilling
Land of *Hypedd*.

So weary traveller
You don't know what's ahead
Turn and run and flee
From the land of *Hypedd!*

John Brady (11)
Holy Family School

Rainy Days

I'm tired of rain and I'm feeling vain
And I'm seeing pain
Every day that it rains
Water flows down the stream
And the roads.
'Oh no' the stream overflows,
How long can I say hey?

Sophie O'Brien (7)
Holy Family School

School

The good thing about school
Is I meet all my friends
But I am sometimes happy
When the school day ends.

I get into line
When the school bell rings
I'm ready to learn
A lot of new things.

I get into class
Sit on the floor
My teacher comes in
Shutting the door.

The boys on my table
Just talk about sport
It wouldn't be good
On their school report.

I quite like maths
And English too
But I'm moving to High School now
What can I do?

I like the teachers
And the whole of the school
And I think that's because
It really is cool!

Helen O'Mara (11)
Holy Family School

In The Sea

The sea is blue but I have the flu
So I'm not allowed in the water!

I shiver and sneeze from the horrible breeze
And I am always sick in bed,
A, a, a, chooo!

Daniel Krause (8)
Holy Family School

All Over The World

All over the world,
There's creatures great and small
All over the world
You can hear them call.

The whistling of the robins
The buzzing of the bees
The munching from the squirrels
These all live in trees.

The giggling of the monkeys
The croaking of the frogs,
The braying of the donkeys
The barking from the dogs.

The roaring of the lions
The purring of the cats
The squawking of the parrots
The muttering of the rats.

The slithering of the snakes
The bleating of the sheep
The neighing of the horses
Eating hay packed in a heap.

All over the world
There's creatures great and small
All over the world
You can hear them call.

Rebecca Chambers (10)
Holy Family School

When I'm At The Sea

When I'm at the sea
Fish go around my knee
They tickle my toes and swim away
All day.

Rachael Bowen (8)
Holy Family School

When I look Out Of The Window

When I look out of the window
I'll tell you what I can see
If it's early in the morning,
The birds nesting in the tree.

When I look out of the window,
I'll tell you what I can spot
Well if I'm in Paris
The Eiffel Tower, why not?

When I look out of the window
I'll tell you what I can see
Well if I'm in New York
Skyscrapers towering over me.

But when I'm back in England
All curled up in my bed
I don't need to look out the window
I've got my imagination instead.

Rachel O'Toole (11)
Holy Family School

Summer

Summer when the sun is so bright
When you look up it's such a beautiful sight
Summer when the birds sing in the breeze
Dandelions in the field make me sneeze.

Lying in my lounge chair in the red hot sun
Drinking a cool drink oh what *fun!*
I'm in my garden having a water fight
The sun is still shining the day is still bright.

But the night comes all too soon
I must go in now here comes the moon!

Caitlin Wynn (10)
Holy Family School

My Class

My class is mad
I don't know why.
My mum and dad
Think it's a lie.

They've hardly ever seen my class,
How lucky I think they are
They've only seen them when they pass
Looking through the car.

Joey smashed the window
Rachel's on the roof,
Who has spilt the water?
David, tell the truth.

Conor spilt the water
But he's strangling the cat
David spilt the water
And that is that!

Becky, please don't eat that
You don't know where it's been
    'It might have been in Amy's mouth.'

Oh Daniel, don't be mean!

Tom it might short circuit
Caitlin don't touch that
Emily take off that coat
I'm sure that's not your hat.

My class is mad
I don't know why
So are my mum and dad
And so am I!

Max Thomas-McGenity (10)
Holy Family School

Wind!

Wind, wind howling wind,
Birds fly off and monkeys swing.

Wind, wind, can push things far
Tidal waves and flying cars.

Wind, wind rips paint off walls
Causes floods and waterfalls.

Wind, wind, blows my hat off my head
It's so strong it blows the quilt off my bed.

Wind, wind blows my friend's shoes off her feet
But lucky for her it blows the dirt off her seat.

Wind, wind, it's driving me mad
If it was sunny I'd be so glad.

No more wind it's driving me so mad
It's so annoying it's making me sad
Tomorrow I'm dying for some sun
I'm honestly hoping the wind will be gone.

Rosie O'Connor (11)
Holy Family School

Football

Football is a really cool game
But most of the girls say it is lame.

Football is very good
When you get full of mud.

Everton is my best team
Ignore Liverpool they are mean.

Chelsea are my favourite team
They go up with a big gleam.

Conor Tiernan (10)
Holy Family School

Robbers

Robbers, robbers, everywhere they could be
Hiding under the stairs.
I get very frightened, I get very scared
Because what if the robber is coming up my stairs.
I shout my mum, I shout my dad
But they don't answer back.
I look in the bathroom, I see a shadow
Oh no it could be the robber Ahhhh.

Robbers, robbers, everywhere, I don't really like them
Because they give me a scare.
They will get you if they need you
So watch out or you're caught.

Robbers, robbers everywhere
They are scary they are scary
So if you're alone be careful,
Because you're in for a scare.
Ha ha ha ha.

Ben Walker (11)
Holy Family School

Homework

H orrible homework I don't like it one bit
O utrageous science revision but
M aybe I'll get a good mark
E xtremely boring history, researching all those dates
W orking for most of the day, and not getting much of a play
O h I wish I didn't have to do it
R unning in the school playground that's far better
  than homework
K ill homework, kill it, I never want to do it again.

Rebecca Murphy (11)
Holy Family School

The Woods

When we last went to the woods
Everyone brought coats with hoods.

When we settled down to camp,
The floor was a little bit too damp.

The next morning it was a sunny day
We all shouted hip, hip, hooray!

It was hotter than ever
We all shouted *never!*

That's what I like best.

Jessica Fogarty (7)
Holy Family School

Friendship

Friendship's made of my best friend
Who always drives me round the bend
This is what he'll always say
What a lovely day
And this is what we always do
We always, always play on PS2.

Glyn Wheeler (7)
Holy Family School

The Sea

The water is blue
And I have the flu
And I lost my shoe
At sea.

Sophie Hilton (8)
Holy Family School

My Garden

My garden is very big
Big enough for a swimming pool to be fitted
Wouldn't that be cool!

I cannot forget the rockery
With bees buzzing all around
By the heather there are some pansies
When you smell them your feet won't
Touch the ground!

Then there is the apple tree,
With apples ever so crunchy!

But when the rain comes
Puddles appear,
They are ever so deep.

But when it freezes,
It is like my garden is sleeping
So soft and white!

So do you like my garden?
I tell you what, I jolly well do!

Rebecca Wilkinson (11)
Holy Family School

Autumn

Autumn is cold
So I've been bold
When leaves blow all over the place
It looks like a big disgrace.

Leaves go crackle, leaves go crunch
While I'm eating my lovely lunch
Red, yellow, brown is the colour they go
Winter will be next and then we'll see snow.

Emily Norris (10)
Holy Family School

Scuba-Diving

S is for scuba-diving like lots of people do
C is for the coral reef where lots of people search
U is for underwater where you go
B is for boats which scuba-divers jump out
A is for apple to keep scuba-divers healthy.

D is for a diving diploma you need
I is for how interesting the fish will be
V is for very exciting like this sport
I is for information you will need to dive
N is for noise the waves will make
G is for guide book you will need to read.

Daniel Dolan (11)
Holy Family School

Rainbows

Rainbows are red like roses that dread.
Rainbows are blue like bluebells that ring with
A ting and a bing.
Rainbows are nice that reminds me of mice
That scamper and skip all day
Rainbows are as high as the sky!

Robbie Sherman (8)
Holy Family School

The Sea On A Sunny Day

The seas are blue
At the sea you can take off your shoes.
It is fun to lay and play in the sun
After a while you can play with the sand
And listen to your favourite bands.

Rachel Howard (8)
Holy Family School

Nature

Roses are red
Violets are blue
Clouds are white
Swamps are dirty
Fountains are squirty
Hunters are smirky
The sky is blue you know too
My football goes into the sky really high
The trees grow larger and larger
Each and every time
Every mine is dug each time.

Joseph Bennett (7)
Holy Family School

Windows

Windows are clean
Like they are seen.
I don't like them all
I do hope they fall
They went splat on the floor
At the top of the wall
What a shame,
They could have been fame.
They were chucked on the dump
Just like a hunk.
It came back to life
Just like a knife
When it shortly came back
It touched Jack
I was so extraordinarily happy
I had to wear a nappy.
Then the window was fuming angry
Just like the royal family.

Paul Sheridan (11)
Holy Spirit Catholic Primary School

The Cat On The Chair

There was a cat who sat on a chair
That's right, that's right, that's right,
He told me that he didn't like to share
And it gave me a bit of a fright
That's right, that's right, that's right.
One night the cat was angry
He chased me round the house
So I ran away, I got a train to Spain
I went to see my friends
They were in Spain.
Goodbye.

Lauren Llewellyn (8)
Holy Spirit Catholic Primary School

My Cousin Your Cousin

My cousin is stronger than your cousin
Well my cousin is strong enough
Well my cousin is bigger than your cousin
Well my cousin is big enough
Well my cousin is better looking than your cousin
Well my cousin is good looking enough
Well my cousin is better at tennis
Well my cousin is good enough at tennis.

Michael O'Brien (7)
Holy Spirit Catholic Primary School

May Is The Month Of Mary

May is the month of Mary
She loves flowers
She loves angels
She loves anything that appears
She is the queen of love.

Stevie Barton (8)
Holy Spirit Catholic Primary School

Sweet As Can Be!

My toffees are amazingly sweet
My disco clothes are extremely neat
I have outstanding meat
My mate has smelly feet
I have outstanding posh seat
For my breakfast I eat shredded wheat
I like a song and it begins with a beat
And when it's really sunny
I can't stand the heat.

Alfie Lyon (11)
Holy Spirit Catholic Primary School

My Cat Ted

My cat Ted
Sleeps on my bed
He has got a cut
In the middle of his head.
My mum said
'Why don't you call it Ned?'
He's incredible
He's just made a shed
But I just love my cat Ted.

Nicole Burrows (8)
Holy Spirit Catholic Primary School

The Old Man

There was an old man
And he bumped his head
Because he fell out of bed
And he had a headache
So he went to the doctors
And the doctor said
'No more falling out of bed.'

Natasha Harrison (8)
Holy Spirit Catholic Primary School

My Aunty Pat

My spotty Aunty Pat
Is extremely tall
I really wish she would fall.

My spotty Aunty Pat
Is so hugely fat
I would burst her
With her cat.

My spotty Aunty Pat
Is so ugly she looks worse
Than my dog Pugly.

My spotty Aunty Pat
Is so thick
I would call doctor Nick.

But the most thing
My spotty Aunty Pat is good at
Is being the goalie because
She's tall and fat.

Hayden Morris (11)
Holy Spirit Catholic Primary School

Spring

All through spring flowers grow
Animals are born
Animals just start to get fur
Flowers go different colours
Even in sheep's hair
The sun is bright it shines like a light
It goes everywhere
Even in my hair
It is so hot people have barbecues
It falls everywhere.

Leoni Picton (8)
Holy Spirit Catholic Primary School

Mrs Kenning

Mrs Kenning is extremely bossy
I've seen her in her cossie
I didn't like the sight
It gave me a fright
Mrs Kenning is extremely bossy.

Mrs Kenning always wears fake hair
I really wouldn't like to stare
If you stare you might get hurt
She's got a son his name is Kurt
My teacher always wears fake hair.

Mrs Kenning is very clever
She's always shouting never
At 9am I see the brace
At 3pm there's a smile on my face
My teacher's very clever.

Mrs Kenning went away
To the island of Duncan Bay
When she came back
We each got a sack
Mrs Kenning went away.

Gemma Coffey (11)
Holy Spirit Catholic Primary School

Hello, Hello

'Hello, hello,' said the lady at the door
'Hello, hello,' answered the man in the store
'I want a delivery for Funny Land
I will come to pick it up in winter.'
'OK we will deliver it
But we don't know where Funny Land is.'
'Not Funny Land,
Bunny Land.'

Shannon Duffy (8)
Holy Spirit Catholic Primary School

My Family

My mum is extremely lovely and nice
And she is always there,
She is a wonderful hairdresser
And she is brilliant at doing hair.

My dad's name is Kenny
And he really likes to sing,
He is always betting on horses
But he never wins a thing.

I have a cute bird called Pipper
Flying is her game
I have another cute little bird
Charlie is his name.

My dog is extremely lazy
He sits by his yummy food each day
Sometimes he can be playful and giddy
And wants to go out and play.

My brother and sister drive me up the wall
They always want their own way
Sometimes I wish my sister
Will leave and run away.

My mum and dad are the best parents
You could wish for
You couldn't wish
For anything more.

Chloe Lever (11)
Holy Spirit Catholic Primary School

My Cousin Your Cousin

My cousin is fatter, your cousin is thinner
My cousin is bigger, your cousin is smaller
My cousin is greedy, your cousin is kinder
My cousin likes football, your cousin likes cricket
My cousin likes toys, your cousin likes boys.

Jon Tuffy (8)
Holy Spirit Catholic Primary School

My Pet

I have a cat
She sits on the mat
Her name is Molly
She looks like a dolly.

She may scratch, she may bite,
If she does you'll get a fright
She's got lots of fur
All over her.

She is stripy and she's warm
But she's scared when there's a storm
She is always fighting
And she's faster than lightning.

She is always lying down
Sometimes she may frown
I have a cat
She sits on the mat.

Hannah Bamber (10)
Holy Spirit Catholic Primary School

Toffee Mad!

A tasty toffee
That's sweet and looks like
Lumps of meat!

A juicy toffee
That's yummy
To have in my big fat tummy.

A scrumptious toffee
That's gummy like jelly
On a dummy!

A savoury toffee
That's chubby but looks very grubby!

Becky Bolton (11)
Holy Spirit Catholic Primary School

The Fox

Walking through a green, grassy meadow,
Was a fox
He was looking for a shelter
Maybe a box.

He had been walking for days
Almost a week
His throat was so dry
He could barely speak.

He knew there wasn't much life for him
Not since the chase
He had barely escaped with a scar
A long one upon his face.

Yet, there in the distance
Was a ginger dot
It was a kindhearted vixen
Who he loved a lot.

He ran limping to her
As she ran across to him,
But when they were a few feet apart
His knees gave in.

'Oh dear what's happened to you?'
The vixen cried
'They were hunting me down'
The fox replied.

The vixen helped him up
So they could walk to her den
They lay down to sleep
Safe from the men.

Heather Boland (11)
Holy Spirit Catholic Primary School

My Friend

M y friend is always caring
Y ou might have a better friend
　 but she is always there for me.

F or years we have known each other
R ound the circle she will always stay to play
I know we will always be friends
E very day she rings to say hi
N ice things happen when we are together
D on't let us fall out.

Gabrielle Critchley (10)
Howick CE Primary School

Vikings

Vikings raid, Vikings trade
Vikings stay up all night
Vikings fight with all their might
Vikings raid land therefore raiding must be banned.

Yasir Mir (8)
Howick CE Primary School

Jack And Jill Vs Miss Muffet

(PS With A Spider In The Poem)

Jack and Jill climbed a hill
And found a bucket of water,
They saw Miss Muffet
And called her a muppet
And scared her away with a spider coming after.

Adam Barnish (8)
Howick CE Primary School

Lovely

Hey, you're lovely
You're so divine
I love you lots
Like a taste of wine.

Lovely you're special
Special to me
You're precious and funny
A pleasure to see.

It's great to walk
With you by my side
In the park
By the slide.

You're funny and sweet
And you're very bubbly
You're cool to be with
You're my dog Lovely.

Emily Whalley (10)
Howick CE Primary School

I'm Scared

I'm scared with the beast inside
When I go on holiday it goes to glide.

I'm scared of the beast inside
When he comes out everyone starts to hide.

I'm scared of the beast within
When he is here I put everything in the bin.

I'm scared of the beast within
When he's about I want to stab him with a pin.

Paris Maddock-Dickinson (9)
Howick CE Primary School

How To Make A Baby Brother

Ingredients
10oz of wanting
40oz of silliness
2oz of strength
3oz of coolness
2oz of craziness
9oz of sleepiness
2oz of racing around.

How to make baby brother
Drop in 4oz of silliness
And sprinkle 2oz of craziness in.
Put 2oz of racing around
To 9oz of sleepiness.
Throw in 3oz of coolness
Lob in 2oz of strength
Drop 10oz of wanting in
Now put it in the oven and leave it
Until it starts screaming
With anger and fury.

Melissa Ross (9)
Kettleshulme St James' CE Primary School

How To Make A Baby Brother

4oz football, 5oz of coolness
6oz of strength, 4oz poopyness
6oz of sickness
Add 4oz of football and 6oz of strength
And stir it for fifteen minutes.
And add 5oz of coolness plus 6oz of sickness
And put it in the oven for at least two whole hours
And take it out and sprinkle more football on the
Mixture and wait for twenty-four hours
And wait for a scream.

Harry Hill (7)
Kettleshulme St James' CE Primary School

How To Make A Super Baby Boy

Ingredients
10 drops of smartness,
A dash of coolness
A handful of your parents slippers,
Your brother's CDs
A pinch of shades
A drop of strength

In goes the slippers, then goes the smartness,
Some CDs and a dash of coolness
Probably some strength and shades
Mix, mix, mix . . . Ta dah!
You've made your mixture, now put it in the oven
Wait for twenty minutes
Hey presto you have a super-powered baby boy.

Dougal Mackenzie (9)
Kettleshulme St James' CE Primary School

How To Make A Baby Sister

Ingredients
1oz crying
A dash of naughtiness
2oz of rudeness
A pinch of spiky hair
8oz of grabbing fingers
10oz of mischievous
6oz sleepiness

Grab a pinch of spiky hair and add some rudeness.
Throw in some grabbing fingers and a dash of naughtiness.
Add some crying and 1oz of mischievous as well as 6oz of sleepiness.
Then put it in the oven until the next day
And then wait until it screams and
After that you are finished.

Anna Townley (7)
Kettleshulme St James' CE Primary School

How To Make A Baby Brother

Ingredients
7oz of sick
A dash of tears
25oz of rude
26oz of mischief
26oz of silly
2 jelly eyeballs.

First put in 7oz of sick
And all the sickly.
Then put in 25oz of rude
And put in 26oz of silly with it.

After put in 26oz of mischief
And make it strong.

Next get 2oz of ear wax with a dash of tears,
Put in 1oz of happy and a pinch of chatterbox.

After all that put it in the oven until it screams
With power take it out
Put on the eyeballs, sprinkle it on the body
And there!

Lorenzo Llull-Grimshaw (8)
Kettleshulme St James' CE Primary School

A Crash Of Waves

In the bright moonlight
The waves crash upon glinting cliffs
Then find a place to settle
Upon whales backs
The whales spray into the moonlit sky
They move away silently
And the shimmering cliffs are wet again.

Lydia Royston (10)
Kettleshulme St James' CE Primary School

How To Make A Baby Sister

Ingredients
A dozen curly hairs
A thousand screams
One slimy shaped heart
And heartbeat
A gallon of hungriness
1oz of niceness
Two round dark blue eyeballs
2000ozs of fatness
60000 freckles
2 rosy red cheeks.

Instructions
Add some of the twelve hairs mix them with the screams
And heart and heartbeat
Add some hungriness and a pinch of niceness
Mix it up
Carefully put the eyeballs in mix with the fatness
And freckles.
Finally put in the cheeks, put in oven and when
Screaming hot you must take them out
It normally takes two hours.

Genna Carr (8)
Kettleshulme St James' CE Primary School

Autumn Time

Season of multicoloured rainbows that glitter like a million stars.
Soft and shining conkers in their beds ready to crack open.
New uniforms bigger than you need
And brand new TV programmes to watch every night.
Birds flying away to some place hot
And harvest which means lots of fruit and veg.
It's nearly winter now with nights turning dark,
'Time to go to bed,' shouts Mum.
Goodnight.

Hollie Theloke (10)
Kettleshulme St James' CE Primary School

The Haunted House

I heard that sound again
What was it?
Since I was about four years old
I had always wanted to go inside.

There were floorboards that creaked
Doors that squeaked
Candles were lit
Vampires that bit!

Pictures with scary eyes, watching your every move,
Funny noises like taps leaking,
Ghosts that floated,
Curtains were coated.

The only thing that would live in this house
Is a very, very brave mouse.

Sophie Hopkin (11)
Kettleshulme St James' CE Primary School

Autumn's Here

Seasons of harvest with golden brown leaves
Picking juicy blackberries
Back to school with a coat too big
Books hungry for writing
Pens with an endless supply of ink
Seeds dispersing all around
Collecting wood for the fire
Packing away summer clothes
Scary masks in shop ready for Hallowe'en
Supermarkets running out of sweets
Trick or treaters on their way.

Autumn's here.

Daisy Tushaw (10)
Kettleshulme St James' CE Primary School

Autumn Days

Season of the rainbow colours
And the rain drizzling down
Harvest of amber and the crunchy leaves
Then the acorns falling off all the trees.

The mellow fruitfulness ripens in the sun
As the fruit grows, day by day, night by night.
Fireworks booming up in the air and *bang*
The fireworks fill the sky with red, orange,
Green and brown.

Blue days and showers as the days pass by.
Apples ripening hour by hour.
Bananas turning colour from green to yellow
To brown.
Best friends dancing around in their warm
Clothes and enjoying.

Emma Booth (9)
Kettleshulme St James' CE Primary School

November

No Santa or Christmas,
No New Year's Day and promises
No Valentines or kisses
No Mother's Day and daffodils
No Easter or newborn chicks
No May Day and dancing
No Father's Day with breakfast in bed
No leavers or leavers' service
No summer holidays with sun, beaches and swimming
No harvest festival or harvest boxes
No Hallowe'en with ghosts and witches
So light the bonfires and watch the fireworks

    It's November!

Jenny Haselwood (11)
Kettleshulme St James' CE Primary School

Seasons

Spring
Snow fades away
Children come out to play
Flowers come out

Summer
Bike rides
Shopping
Sunny days by
The pool

Autumn
Leaves come down
And change golden brown
Flowers die 'Oh no.'

Winter
Snow falls down
Grass disappears
Make snowmen

'Yippee!' What fun we had this year.

Megan Jackson (9)
Kettleshulme St James' CE Primary School

My Friend

She's glue sticking to me
She's a vulture swooping around me
She's a magnet attracting me
She's a vine grabbing on to me
She's a dog not leaving me alone
She's a lion chasing me like its prey
She's a gargling waterfall, which never stops
She's a golden retriever fetching things
She's fizzy lemonade about to explode
She's a dog that never gets tired.

Taylor McDonald-Webb (10)
Kettleshulme St James' CE Primary School

How To Make A Baby Sister

So you want to know how to make a baby sister?
Here's how.
First you need the ingredients
4oz of sugar, spice and everything nice
1oz of screaming
6oz of glaring and beaming
A drop of naughtiness
Her hair has to be a mess.

Get a bowl
Add the screaming
Mix it with the glaring and beaming
Put in a drop of naughtiness
Also poke in the sugar, spice and everything nice.

Becky Lisle (8)
Kettleshulme St James' CE Primary School

The Very Confused Little Girl

I am feeling rather funny
I am feeling rather weird
I woke up just this morning
To find I'd grown a beard.

I'm feeling rather loopy
I'm feeling rather queer
I woke up just this morning
With hair growing from my ear.

I'm feeling rather batty
I'm feeling rather mad
I woke up just this morning
To find I was a lad.

Things are getting strange
Things are getting hotter
I wonder what I have done
To anger Harry Potter.

Katie Whyte (10)
Kew Woods Primary School

Good But Bad

It's finally come,
It's exceedingly near,
No more arguing at night,
But Dad won't be here.

He's moving away,
He's already filed,
Mum's usually calm,
But now she's gone wild.

She's lost her touch in cleaning,
The kitchen's like a sty,
Why did this happen
Oh why, oh why, oh why?

Some parents are lovebirds,
They never even shout
They always get on,
And dance and prance about.

But my parents aren't like this,
They drive me round the bend.
Though I'm upset about it,
At last this feud will end.

Jodie Altham (10)
Kew Woods Primary School

My Funny Little Ghost
(Dedicated to Uncle Mark who sadly passed away)

I have a funny little ghost in my house,
And it's scared of my little pet mouse,
And when I go out,
It moves things about,
And it eats strange ugly bugs and louse.

Jessica Fletcher (9)
Kew Woods Primary School

The Fair

When I go to the fair I love it there
I go up and down side to side left and right
I go on the dodgems
I dodge left to right
I hit other cars and have a fright
I go on the Ferris wheel and I look down
Guess what I can see? A clown
Next I go to the burger bar I have a nice juicy burger
And a cold can
Then I go to the rollercoaster
When I get on I feel nervous
I go down the steep hill the wind blows in my face
And gives me a chill.

Now it's time to go I feel really sad
But I know I've got to go.

Aaron Lovelady (10)
Kew Woods Primary School

Once Upon A Spirit . . .

The spirits are arising,
All around the room,
Don't let the evil come
In the ancient tomb,
The spirits are arising,
Come out from everywhere,
The evil has the power,
In its secret lair,
Out from the vase,
The spirits will come,
After the day is over,
The job will be done,
The day is over,
The moonlight has shone,
The spirits have arisen,
The evil has come.

Molly Bryson (10)
Kew Woods Primary School

The Upside Down Divorce

Why can't they be together?
All because of a stupid row,
Two homes I live in now,
It's all right for my sister,
She's got Dad,
I'm stuck with Mum.
I slave for her all day,
Never a thank you,
It's always 'You could do better.'
I only see him at weekends,
I miss Dad
Since they s p l i t I cry at night,
Everyone's sticking up for Mum,
I'm on Dad's side.
It was Mum's fault but nobody believes me.
I hate divorce!

Jenny Craggs (11)
Kew Woods Primary School

Oh Water, Oh Water

Oh water, oh water falling from the sky
Oh water, oh water rushing down the stream.

Oh water, oh water, crashing over the waterfall,
Oh water, oh water trickling through my fingers.

Oh river, oh river pushing logs and stones along
Oh river, oh river meandering around and around the bends.

Oh river, oh river so clean and clear
Oh river, oh river so fast and slow.

Christopher Benson (11)
Kew Woods Primary School

Basketball

Basketball, basketball, bounce so high
Basketball, basketball, goes in the net
Home team score up
Visitors score behind.

Oh . . . how are we winning
Oh . . . how are we winning
I think we're the best!

Fly ball fly get in
Yes! What a throw!
Come on 52-1 home
I spoke too soon!

Oh . . . now it is 52-2 home,
Oh . . . but we are still winning,
We think they're the worst!

There goes the whistle
Of course we won! We're the best!
When we got to the changing rooms,
We weren't even sweaty.

Alex Couzens (9)
Kew Woods Primary School

In The Style Of Michael Rosen

For Mum
I'm the kind of son who
My parents don't want to be
Seen with because . . .

I'm the kind of son
Who plays too much football
Sings in the bath
Never flushes the loo
Smashes too many windows
Won't bother tidying my room
And fights with his sister.

Mark McNorton (11)
Kew Woods Primary School

I Think School Is Boring

I think school is boring
I mean you have to do maths
In a stuffy old class
And do things that make everyone yawn.

But when it comes to English
Which is a favourite subject of mine
I think it's OK, right then it's fine
Because my best subject is English.

I like Art and DT
And Geography
Music and singing
(But I hate it when the school bell is ringing).

Maybe school isn't a bore
And maybe I like maths
Even though it's in a stuffy old class
And even things that make you yawn.

Sophie Altham (8)
Kew Woods Primary School

Monstrosity

I saw a monster in the fridge
This thing was hairy
This thing was ugly
This thing was big
This thing had ten eyes
And they were all looking right at me
I saw a monster in the cupboard
This thing was very hairy
This thing was grotesque
This thing was huge
This thing had twenty eyes
And they were all looking right at me.

Kristian Roylance (11)
Kew Woods Primary School

My Hamster

Today my hamster sat up in bed
And while she did
I stroked her head
She went round in her wheel
And while she did
I was watching a Catherine wheel.

Today my hamster was making her bed
And while she did
I got fed
She ate her food as quick as that
And while she did
My sister spat.

Today my hamster is drinking water
And while she did
In comes my aunty's daughter.

Today my hamster sat up in bed
And while she did
I stroked her head.

Abby Makin (8)
Kew Woods Primary School

There's A Monster Under My Bed

There's a monster under my bed
And I think it's the colour red
It acts like a dog
And it's got the attention span of a log
Once I found out
That it had ate a sprout
I looked under my bed
And now I'm dead.

John Steel (11)
Kew Woods Primary School

The Boy At School

I was teasing a boy today,
I called him names and chanted,
His face was in dismay,
My friends all laughed and grinned.

My friends and me were laughing,
At what we did first play,
I started to feel bad inside,
At the end of the day.

While at home on the PS2,
I started to think what I should do,
I thought I should apologise,
And say sorry for all those lies.

I went to school the next day,
I thought he'd be there in dismay,
But to my shame he wasn't there,
And all my friends didn't care.

Jordan Crowney (10) & Philip Weston (11)
Kew Woods Primary School

Dog

Bum sniffing
Bone eating
Public pooing
Age dying
Wash hating
Cool styling
Walk loving
Tree exploring
Tail wagging.

Lynn Koworera (10)
Kew Woods Primary School

In The Silence Of The Night

In the silence of the night
When the north wind blows
Just out of sight
The leaves rustle in the wind
And the tree branches crack onto a phone line
Down from the hills
Down from the lake
Something hideous appears by magic
The owls go 'tu-whit tu-whoo' as if they're screaming to a popstar.

In the silence of the night
Marks on trees disappear
And death is written on the trees in blood
Poisonous snakes cast *venom* on its prey
And because of the phone lines nobody can get through
And rats are dying because of the snakes
So are bugs and flies
Because of the snakes no one dares go in
Leaves are brown and dying
Birds never go in.

Kieran Rigby (8)
Kew Woods Primary School

Cat

Tail flapper
Door scratcher
Long sleeper
Graceful eater
Fence jumper
Pole scratcher
Milk taster
Public fur ball
Fish feeder
Door mouse devourer
Mouse mincher
Peaceful pet.

Jordan Sudlow-Lane (10)
Kew Woods Primary School

The Never-Ending Argument

They've done it again,
They've had an argument
Dad has to leave
He says I can live with him,
Mum says I have to live with her.

I try to sneak away,
But my nasty sister tells her.
She goes extremely mad,
And says it's my dad's fault,
I know it's not.

My dad begs my mum to let me live with him,
She turns into a maniac,
And calls the police.
Dad gets arrested,
Through no fault of his own.

I have a big argument with Mum
She sends me to my room,
Because she has had enough of me,
She sends me into care,
Which I am not glad about.

I beg Alice (the lady in the orphanage),
To let me live with my dad,
She gets really annoyed
And sends me to live with my dad,
Me and my dad live happily ever after.

Ahh! Isn't that nice?

Naomi Wilson (11)
Kew Woods Primary School

In My Jungle

In my jungle there is a tiger with no stripes,
A giraffe with no spots,
A lion with no mane,
A monkey without a mate,
An ape tied in sellotape,
An elephant with no shape,
A rhino with a trunk,
A hippo with no mouth,
A crocodile with no teeth,
A porcupine with no spines,
A snake eating chocolate,
A koala bear eating candyfloss
A zebra that is pink and purple
A buffalo that is blue
Bugs that are red
And a parrot that's lost its squawk.

Laura Eyes (10)
Kew Woods Primary School

The Assassination Of Confidence

Bullies can grind you,
You will end up feeling so meaningless
That you will have no confidence left at all.
Bullies seem to have an additional power,
That will prickle your forehead;
Wherever . . . you . . . go!

There is an unstoppable force
Projected by a bully
That forces fear to overcome you!

> The way to resist
> Is . . . unknown!

Jonathan Howard & Dean Orme (10)
Kew Woods Primary School

Dad's Gone

Dad's gone
Said he would call
Never did though
Never has.

I wait by the phone
All day after school
When the phone rings I answer
'Dad'
But it's not you.

Why did you go Dad?
Without saying goodbye
But something's become sad Dad
I can't remember what you look like.

It was a stormy night when he left
In the winter times of December
You missed Christmas Dad
I miss you so much Dad.

So I will carry on waiting Dad
Next to the phone
Waiting and waiting
Hoping you will call.

Chloe Campbell (11)
Kew Woods Primary School

My Dad

My dad is mad
He really is,
He's very jokeful
And he loves to trick me.
When we
Go out he embarrasses me,
That's my dad
I like him lots!

Rebecca Jones (11)
Kew Woods Primary School

Contamination

Chimney works and all it leaves is
Smoke, smoke and smoke.
Cars work and all they leave is
Smoke, smoke and smoke.
Trucks, motorcycles, buses work
And all they leave are smoke.

Petroleum in the sea
Cigarettes everywhere,
Global warming is close
And there are no trees enough,
So . . .

How do you expect that the Earth is going to
Live a thousand years more if we are destroying it?

Take care of it,
She needs you.

Isabel Miranda N (11)
Kew Woods Primary School

In The Whole Wide World

In the whole wide world
There is a . . .

Sky full of clouds,
A rainbow full of colours,
Planets big and small,
Flowers dead or alive,
Rivers full of fish,
Jungles full of trees,
Animals striped or plain,
And people bright or silly.

Siân Davies (9)
Kew Woods Primary School

The World At Night!

The stars are bright,
Just like my might,
As I turn off the lights,
On the dark up nights.
I look around,
But I don't hear a sound.
Then when I start to curl,
I see my auntie Pearl.
The birds start to tweet,
And I think it's so sweet.
The dog jumps up,
As I smash my cup
Everything goes scary
As I get wary
I feel like I'm dead
So I better go to bed!

Victoria Hannah (10)
Kew Woods Primary School

The Giant Flea

One day my friend said to me,
'Look! What do you see?'
There in a pool
Was something cool,
There was a giant flea!

It was the biggest thing I'd ever seen,
And I said, 'It really needs a clean.'
And the flea said,
'I need to be fed.'
And I whisper, 'I hope it's not mean!'

Daniel Lloyd (10)
Kew Woods Primary School

Choosing

Which to choose?
Who shall I live with?
Mum or Dad?

Then Mum
Says to me
'Treat yourself to what you want
But don't spend it all at once.'

So when I was a spoilt kid
I started to think
'Why am I this lucky?'
And then I realised Mum wants me more.

So now I have to choose
What I want to do
I think I've made my decision
Put me in the orphanage!

Stuart Eyes & Meghan Standeven (11)
Kew Woods Primary School

In My Zoo!

In my zoo there's an ape tied in sticky tape
A monkey without a banana
A giraffe with many pink spots
A tiger without a stripe
An elephant with no trunk
A rhino with no horn
Some birds that really can't sing
A snake with no forked tongue
In my zoo everything seems to go
Completely wrong!

Amber Williams (11)
Kew Woods Primary School

They Were Having A Divorce!

My dad left when I was five
He didn't come back at all
My mum would cry and so would I
Then there was the call.

They were having a divorce!

He came around and got his stuff
I thought he'd stay forever
I blamed myself but now I know
They just weren't happy together.

They were having a divorce!

I had to go to the council
And stand in front of judges,
I had to choose where to go,
My clear lines have all smudges.

They were having a divorce!

Jonathan Foster & Andrew Lea (11)
Kew Woods Primary School

Dog

Fast runnin'
Bone lickin'
Eye shimmin'
Body scratchin'
Paw givin'
Tail waggin'
Pavement sniffin'
Bum shakin'
Cat hatin'
Dog!

Lisa Jackson (10)
Kew Woods Primary School

I Feel Big

I kicked little Bill's ball over the fence,
Then I kicked and punched him.
I feel immense.

Everyone is petrified of *me* in *my* school,
I force out their dinner money.
I feel cool.

I nicked Sally's trip money
And spent it with my mate
We laughed and pointed at her.
I feel great.

Little Jim is crying 'cause I called him a pig,
I am big Bob and I feel big.

Rory Boyer (10) & Joseph Moran (11)
Kew Woods Primary School

What Am I?

Long brown swishing tail,
A body as black as night,
Gleaming nose, so pink and frail,
Gallops as fast as the speed of light.

Rolling in the crisp green grass
Coat shimmering in the light,
He rushes across the golden sand
Leaving hoof prints out of sight.

Flying mane blows against the gentle breeze
As he canters through the crowded wood
Emerging to the high tide ocean.

    What am I?

Katy Burgess-Cox (11)
Kew Woods Primary School

Isolated

Divorce was enough
But not for the judges
Holding grudges, against us

Bang!

Went the gavel
That destroyed our home
Now our only contact was by phone.

Dad's gone now
Mum has to flee
I'm with children in the same situation as me.

I'm sitting on the window sill
Isolated from others
Waiting to see my father and my mother

Social workers made a fuss
Since no one got custody
Was it because no one wanted me?

Isolated all alone.

Chowa Nkonde (10)
Kew Woods Primary School

Star Of The Week

Star of the week
Is like eating meat
Whatever the name
The lesson is always the same.

If you're always good
You will get a piece of the pud
So try your best
You just might beat the rest.

Billy Brookfield (9)
Kew Woods Primary School

A Poem From A Bully's Point Of View

Walter is top in all his classes,
And he wears the geekiest glasses.
His nose has got lots of spots,
I changed his pen so he'd write in blots.

He wears the biggest braces,
And wears clothes with frilly laces.
He spends his time reading books,
And people skit his bad looks.

I always nick Walter's money,
And other people think it's funny.
Yesterday I beat him up,
Plus I gave him an uppercut.
He went to the teacher and told on me,
And then the teacher sent for me.

Ryan Burgess (10) & Curtis Rigby (11)
Kew Woods Primary School

I Feel

I feel like an angry lion,
Roaring like Dad did before he left.

I feel like a lonely mouse alone in a hole,
Like my most prized possession has been
Taken in a theft.

I feel like a quiz book with so many questions,
Not answered in my confusion.

I feel like a science experiment,
With no conclusion.

I feel like my heart will be broken,
Until Dad returns again.

Chloe Fitton (10) & Mohammed Osman (11)
Kew Woods Primary School

Stuck In The Middle

I'm stuck in the middle,
And don't know what to do.
My mum doesn't want me,
And my dad doesn't too.

'Go with your mum!'
'Go with your dad!'
That's what they say
They are equally bad.

It's all right for sis.
Both of them want her.
But what about me?
I'll be put into care!

When they were together
Everything was great.
We all played together
By the garden gate.

But now it's changed
And I'm all alone.
My parents don't want me
I'm on my own.

Jack Widdison & Amy Moore (11)
Kew Woods Primary School

Wilcock Bert

There once was a lady called Wilcock Bert
And every day she wears a multicoloured skirt
She flies through the day and the night
And she's got a terrible bite.

Her best friend is a bear
He's got white hair
He will give you a scare
That's her bear.

Daniel Lea (9)
Kew Woods Primary School

Bullying

I bullied a boy called Tim today
My friends started to laugh
He started to cry
And ran away down the path.

Back in the classroom
My friends started to tease Tim
He looked sad and miserable
Now I felt sorry for him.

When I got home
I imagined Tim shrinking
I was angry and frustrated
I just couldn't stop thinking.

The next day at school
I apologised to him
A girl had told off me
She said I had teased Tim!

Adam Monk (10) & Amro Mohamed (11)
Kew Woods Primary School

My Naughty Friend

My naughty friend is so bad
She runs around the block like mad.

She was normally good
But she never ate her pud.

But then she got crazy
She mooed like Daisy.

But then she got good
But she still never ate her pud.

Bobbie-Rose Warran (9)
Kew Woods Primary School

Lunch Boxes, Munch Boxes

Lunch boxes, munch boxes
Yellow, black, blue
I've got cheese sandwiches
How about you?

Lunch boxes, munch boxes
Purple, silver, gold
What's in your sandwiches?
Because I've got mould.

Lunch boxes, munch boxes
Green, black, yellow
All I've got is a big
Marshmallow.

Lunch boxes, munch boxes
Blue, yellow, green
For my afters I've got
Strawberries and cream.

Mathew Earle (8)
Kew Woods Primary School

Who Am I?

Goal kicker
Ball flicker

Rule breaker
Corner taker

Penalty shooter
What a booter

Hairstyle changer
Right foot danger!

Tattoo mania
Football insania

Who am I?

Stephen Roberts (11)
Kew Woods Primary School

Animals Everywhere

Animals, animals
I like animals
They run
They walk
I like animals.

Monkeys, monkeys
Hang from trees
Dance around
Like flying bees
That's my monkey.

Cheetah, cheetah
Run like thunder
Eat you up
And never mutter
That's my cheetah.

Penguins, penguins
Splash you all
Never would hurt you
They play with a ball
That's my penguin.

Sophie Wood (9)
Kew Woods Primary School

Dolphin

Swim dolphin swim fast
Swim dolphin through the ocean
Blaze through the blue sea
Be as happy as can be.

Hannah Golland (9)
Kew Woods Primary School

Hamsters

Today I saw a hamster
Running in his ball
Playing in his bedroom
I can't believe how small.

Today I saw a hamster
Asleep in his bed
I can't believe he got to sleep so quick
Oh hurt your head.

Today I saw a hamster
Playing by the door
Doesn't know where to go
Oops trapped his toe in the door.

Today I saw a hamster
He got stuck in his cage
So he fell asleep and I got him out
I was reading a book,
Oops he got stuck on a page.

Jade Muncaster (8)
Kew Woods Primary School

My Elephant

My elephant is not very fierce,
But he has great big ears,
And sometimes fears,
He made friends with deers.

He goes whoop,
And can count to two,
With a great big nose
And three toes.

With four big feet
Eats a lot of wheat
He is very big
But doesn't wear a wig.

Connor Morris (9)
Kew Woods Primary School

Hamsters

Today I saw a hamster
Running in his ball
He was running in my bedroom
He looked very small.

Today I saw a hamster
Asleep in his bed
Imagine when he woke up
He really banged his head.

Today I saw a hamster
Running on the floor
He didn't know where to go
So he ran round even more.

Today I saw a hamster
Looking round my house
I'm glad he's not a cat
Killing my brother's mouse.

Jade Brothers (8)
Kew Woods Primary School

I Don't Know What To Do

My dog was stolen by a mean old lady
Who is always mean to me
She is only mean because her face is green
And now she's taking it out on me.
I don't know what to do
Oh poo, oh poo.
All because she needed the loo
And now I don't know what to do
Oh poo, oh poo.
I really wanted to play all day, all day,
I really wanted to play.

Rebecca Moorhouse (9)
Kew Woods Primary School

My Wacky Aunty's animals

My aunty's really wacky
Wacky she is.
She has all kinds of animals
Dolphins that can drink fizz.

My aunty's really wacky
What the heck is she?
She has all kinds of animals
Seals open a door with a key.

My aunty's really wacky
She's got a whole show
She's got all kinds of animals
Zebras that can sow.

My aunty's really wacky
You should know it all
She's got all kinds of animals
Penguins that can catch a ball.

Sarah Murray (9)
Kew Woods Primary School

It Was So Calm

It was so calm that I could hear
The door handle creak
As it opened.

It was so calm that I could hear
My pencil rustle
On the paper.

It was so calm that I could hear
The plastic bag rustle
As it floated off.

It was so calm that I could hear
Rock muscle
For space.

Matthew Powell (8)
Kew Woods Primary School

Sports

I like sports
And other things too.
I like football
How about you?

I like tennis and football
And very good sports
Man U beat Millwall
In most sports they wear shorts.

Tennis is very good
I like it very much
I like tennis balls
It's good to touch.

I play sports all the time
I like them
It's my rhyme
I watch sports with my friend Ben.

James Bailey (8)
Kew Woods Primary School

Football Crazy!

Football crazy is all I like,
I watch it every Sunday
When my sister's
On her bike.

When they score
All I see
David Beckham running
Down the pitch like me.

The whistle blows
Fireworks go up
We scored just in time
To win the World Cup.

Harry Standeven (9)
Kew Woods Primary School

My Sister

I hardly ever see my sister
She sings to the radio
And old bagpipes.

I cannot sleep when she twists and twirls
She's like an elephant
I wish I was an only child
Because my sister's wild.

I wake up, bags under my eyes
She eats five hundred tigers
In a pretty dream
With sugar and cream
And my blister of a sister is gone.

If I shared a room with her
I would probably crack
I would rather sleep in a sack
Than with my sister.

Bethany Clarke (9)
Kew Woods Primary School

My Family

My family are the best
They are the best at chess
Everyone snores like mad
But not as bad as my dad.
He has two scars on both hands
But that doesn't mean he can't watch rock bands.

My mum is cool
She wears a lot of jewels
She tries to stop animal killers
Because she loves gorillas.

Michael James Casey (9)
Kew Woods Primary School

My Garden

The air is fragranced around me,
A few steps in front of me,
I could see a water fountain,
With the water falling in a soothmic rhythm.
The sound of birds tweeting filled my heart with joy.
I could also feel the grass as soft as feathers
Beneath me,
To my right there's a group of butterflies
Flying up and down,
Like a bird swooping for prey,
While on my left the sound of children happily
Slurping ice creams could be heard.
If I listened carefully I could just hear the
Sound of church bells ringing in the distance.
The smell of hot dogs on a barbecue, teased my nose.
I felt sensational in my garden.

Elise Bryson (10)
Kew Woods Primary School

Who Am I?

I have a collar,
A litter tray, a toy mouse,
Food and a drink.
I wonder around everywhere
I have a flap and play with my friends,
I have a scratch mat,
My friends do too.
I love being stroked and tickled,
I sleep anywhere around the house
And put hairs everywhere.

      Who am I?

Anastasia Price (10)
Kingsway Primary School

Roll Up, Roll Up

Roll up, roll up,
Come and play,
Roll up, roll up,
You don't have to pay,
Roll up, roll up,
I am starving,
Roll up, roll up
I am halving,
Roll up, roll up,
What shall we eat?
Roll up, roll up,
I'll eat meat,
Roll up, roll up,
What's today?
Roll up, roll up,
It's my birthday,
Roll up, roll up,
Be happy,
Roll up, roll up,
Wear your nappy,
Roll up, roll up,
What's your name?
Roll up, roll up,
My name is Jane,
Roll up, roll up,
My age is nine,
Roll up, roll up,
Of course I'm fine,
Roll up, roll up,
I like school,
Roll up, roll up,
Because it's cool.

Amal Ahmed (10)
Kingsway Primary School

Season Haikus

Spring is . . .
A sign of new life
Molten sun in deep blue sea
Dancing butterflies.

Summer is . . .
Waves crashing on rocks
Clear sky, blazing hot sunlight
As tides grow higher.

Autumn is . . .
Smell of frosty air
Cool, icy, swirling frosty wind,
Floating leaves off ground.

Winter is . . .
Snow drifting to Earth
Creating large snow angels
Warm wrapped up children.

Davie Dunlop (11)
Kingsway Primary School

Dad Shows On TV

My dad watches all sorts of things
And when he watches cartoons he laughs
When he listens to music he sings.

My dad watches football
He wants them to score,
When they do, he goes up the wall.

My dad watches the forecast
They say it will be good
But you know it won't last
But the lawn is soggy mud.

Paul Lloyd (9)
Kingsway Primary School

A Fairground Is . . .

The sight of a roller coaster
Going up and down
And lights on the big wheel.

The sound of children
Screaming on the swinging ship
And laughing in the house of mirrors.

The taste of candyfloss
Melting in your mouth.

The smell of hot dogs
Sizzling on the grill
And cheese melting on burgers.

The touch of a balloon
Slipping through your fingers
And drifting up into the sky.

Michael Davis (10)
Kingsway Primary School

What Am I?

My name is Bugsy
I've got long ears
Also huge teeth
Mostly I eat veg
But sometimes eat fruit
I just love hopping through the trees
I can live in a house or out in the wild
Or I can live in a cage in a backyard
What am I?

Alexandra Lewis (10)
Kingsway Primary School

A Haiku Yearbook

Spring is . . .
Flowers finally
Have burst out of their cages
Gasping breaths of air.

Summer is . . .
Kids laugh whilst they are
Playing on reflecting slides
Looking at the sun.

Autumn is . . .
Autumn makes all trees
Get rid of their crispy egg
Shaped discarded leaves.

Winter is . . .
Slippery ice which
Is freezing everywhere whilst
Most animals flee.

Jenna Griffiths (11)
Kingsway Primary School

Tomb Tune

Here lies the body of Liam Gravett
And if you forget it you're going to regret it
So here I am writing a rhyme
Because I got blamed for a crime
I didn't do.
Why? would I eat someone's shoe
Then they said I blew up the moon
But it wasn't me it was June
That didn't happen because I'm just
Sitting here tapping!

Liam Gravett (10)
Kingsway Primary School

One Whole Year

Buds beginning to show
Flowers are showing their hands
Gardens are coming back.

Taste of cold ice cream
Waves crashing on the shore
Hot all day long.

Leaves are off the trees
Walks through parks
Leaves are crunching
Bare trees nothing to see.

Wearing warm jumpers
Tops of ponds are frozen
Clouds are everywhere.

Jennie May (11)
Kingsway Primary School

Season Haiku

Extraordinary flowers
Start rising in the season spring
Pollens collected.

Excitement's all around
But people swim in water
Some sand is soggy.

Crunchy autumn leaves
They spin in the see-through air
Hitting the hard ground.

Different shaped snowflakes
In streets we play snowball fights
Absolutely cold.

Michael Wookey (11)
Kingsway Primary School

Summer Begins

Summer begins
Sun cracking the flags
Refreshing taste of ice cream
Scent of gleaming sand.

Winter begins
Touch of solid snow
Smell of hot fire burning
Taste of icy snow.

Autumn begins
Crunchy autumn leaves
Rotate in the deep blue sky
Waving a goodbye.

Spring begins
Daffodils risen
Kids diving in crunchy leaves
Trees begin to cry.

Ryan Bradley (11)
Kingsway Primary School

Seasons Haiku

Frosty white snowflakes
Bare barked trees dressed with white snow
Be good for Santa.

Flowers are sprouting
Spring is a wonderful thing
With little lamb legs.

Taste the salty sea
With new fresh smell of doughnuts
In great summer air.

Crunching grass with leaves
Things are getting cold this season
Falling golden leaves.

Matthew Bowie (11)
Kingsway Primary School

The Haiku Seasons

Summer is . . .
Hot sun in the sand
As ice cream melts on pebbles
Parents bathe in sun.

Winter is . . .
Winter's very cold
In winter we wrap up warm
Snow falls in winter.

Autumn is . . .
Animals habitats move
Leaves start to fall off the trees
Squirrels collect food.

Spring is . . .
Daffodils start to grow
Animals come out of their habitats
Birds fly in the spring.

Kayleigh Pinch (11)
Kingsway Primary School

Seasons Haiku

Plants grow through spring
Bright flowers sprout from sown seeds
Like hares from burrows.

Summer water shines
As waves rise into blue sky
Like a wall rising.

Dry leaves on the ground
Green apples spread on the Earth
Autumn is here.

Winter snowball fight
Hot chocolate by a warm fire
Looking out too cold.

Jack Mercer (11)
Kingsway Primary School

Seasons Haiku

Summer Is . . .
Surfing in the sun
Kids jumping on the smooth sand
While hot dogs bake.

Spring is . . .
Robins fly to feed
Spring leaves beginning to grow
When lovely spring comes.

Autumn is . . .
Leaves fall on soft ground
Most animals hibernate
And gather some food.

Winter is . . .
Winter roast turkey
Snowball fights all of the time
And fun snow angels.

Christopher Carson (11)
Kingsway Primary School

Who Am I?

I pounce and scratch
But really I'm cuddly
You'll think I'm cute
I'm no good with dogs.

You probably think I'm like a dalmation
My white body and black patches
But I don't like dogs
They're horrible brutes.

I like fish and mice
I've got sharp claws
I'd wreck your furniture
Guess what I am?

Jordan McWilliams (10)
Kingsway Primary School

What Am I?

I swish my tail in the wind
A party game where my tail is pinned
A variety of colours
My tail comes straight, curly and permed.

I am always really sweaty
After wearing my small tight dressage saddle
My numrah is really comfy
I never feel anyone on my back.

I swiftly move my long legs
Jumping high and stretching my muscles straight
Pat my leg to see my hooves
Thin or fat, small and tall, wide and stumpy legs.
What am I?

Amelia Jenkins (10)
Kingsway Primary School

Tigers

Tigers are cute, furry animals
They wander around the jungle
I wish I could be a tiger
Or have one as my pet.

People say they have flat faces
But I think they are rather cute
I wish they weren't dangerous
So I could have one as my friend.

They are big, bold and strong
They are fast, sometimes slow
They have thick and stripy fur,
They have sharp teeth but I still like them.

Sian Mason (10)
Kingsway Primary School

Pets

My dog is so lazy
His tail is so long
He is so crazy
He always does something wrong.

My parrot is so grey
He can talk
He can build out of clay
And skateboard like Tony Hawk.

Liam Bradley (9)
Kingsway Primary School

Who Am I?

I'm Joey a member of the parrots
You can buy me as a pet
I can spread my wings and soar
All of us come with bright red rosy cheeks
Stroke my head and receive a kiss
My beak can crack a nut
I have got little legs that carry me along branches
Feed me on sunflower seeds and water.
    Who am I?

Jake Parrott (10)
Kingsway Primary School

Love

Love tastes of strawberries in your mouth
It feels like a heart pumping for joy
Love sounds like a song
It smells like chocolate cooking on the stove
And it's romantic.

Lauren Randall (10)
Kingsway Primary School

Baby Callum

Baby Callum's feet are so sweet,
When you tickle them he thinks it's neat,
When he goes in the bath he has a real laugh,
With all the bubbles he causes trouble,
Splishing and sploshing he makes a real mess
What do you think Mum says?
I think you can guess,
He is my baby brother he makes me smile,
But if you see him coming you better run a mile.

Abbie Read (8)
Nether Kellett Community Primary School

Lazy Afternoons

L ying down, licking a lolly,
A nimals bleating in the distance
Z zz go the bees above my head
Y oyos whirling in my brother's hand.

A unty Angie sipping her lemonade,
F eeling warm in the burning sun
T ennis rackets by my side for later
E veryone without a care in the world
R elaxing in the paddling pool
N eeding a wipe for my sticky palms
O ozing sun cream out of the bottle
O range, yellow, the colours of the sun
N othing to worry about on a lazy afternoon!

James Becker (9)
North Cheshire Jewish Primary School

Winter Wonderland!

The cold and icy weather doesn't change at all
The love and enjoyment of the snowy fall
As layers of frost cover the land
A winter wonderland comes into hand.

Beautiful cracked patterns glazed into the ice
Perfect for skating all slippery and nice
Snowball fights all through the day
Birds hide in their nests, Robin and Jay.

There's Frosty the snowman with stones for eyes
When the clean and dry weather fades and dies.
And children happily play together
Oh what a happy time is the winter weather.

The next morn Mr Glacier arrives
No more snow, no more fun, glacier deprives
No more frost, no more cold
A wintry tale now finished and told.

But a sort of compromise you will see
The wintry weather's secrets now revealed for me.
No longer kept beneath the ice and snow
Secrets spread everywhere, high up and below.

Even so, next winter season watch and play
Ignore parent's calls all the day
But the snow won't last forever
Though it's painful blizzards whirl and blast!
The snow does have some good points
So please enjoy it while it lasts!

Jemma Becker (10)
North Cheshire Jewish Primary School

The World Around Me

The world around me is so big,
I never knew how big it was,
The clouds are so floatable,
Are they made out of marshmallows?
Then I ask myself who created English?
Then I realise so many mysteries.
I can't figure them all out.
Then I say I love *life!*

Talya Lewis (9)
North Cheshire Jewish Primary School

Down In The Staff Room
(Based on Michael Rosen's 'Down Behind The Dustbin')

Down in the staff room
I met a teacher called Miss Wood
'What are you doing?' I said
'Unlike you what I should!'

Down in the staff room
I met a teacher called Mrs Core
'No time to talk,' she said
'I'm trying to plan a war.'

Down in the staff room
I met a teacher called Mrs Barry
'Please can you help me?' I asked
'Sorry I've got enough to carry.'

Down in the staff room
I met a teacher called Mrs Field
'Can I help you with those letters?' I asked
'Sorry they're all sealed.'

Down in the staff room
I met a teacher called Mrs Soane
'Not now dear,' she said
'I'm on the phone.'

Emily Gandy (9)
Our Lady's RC Primary School

The Winter

The wind blew,
With its icy breath,
Whistling a damp, dark tune
The trees shivered
As the wind swept past
Under the light of the moon.

The sun comes up
And the hail goes down
Jumping along the streets.
The stones trembled
As the hail stomped down
In the cold winter sun.

The spring rises
From its wintry bed
And wipes the cold away
She puts up a fight
And the winter in fright
Crawls away 'til another day.

Rachael Galilee (11)
Our Lady's Catholic Primary School

Leighton Anderson

I am as thin as a stick
I am as fit as a flea
I am as big as a tree
I am as happy as a clown
And I am as flat as a door.

I am as clever as a computer
I am as hot as a kettle
I am as fast as a cheetah
I am as white as snow.

Leighton Anderson (10)
Our Lady's Catholic Primary School

The Storm

I hear a pitter-patter at my window
I feel the cold air blowing at my face
The trees blow wildly as if at any moment,
They could break.
The storm is making his appearance,
He is as angry as a roaring lion.
He is getting stronger and stronger,
I must take shelter
Until the storm has passed through.

Connor Taylor (11)
Our Lady's Catholic Primary School

The Snow

In the winter when it snows
It's cold and nothing grows
Cold wind nipping at your nose
Wet snow freezing all my toes.

Snow is silent, snow is soft,
I will feel better when it has cleared off.
Snow, I wish you'd go away
The sun comes out, goodbye snow.

Kimberley Darbyshire (11)
Our Lady's Catholic Primary School

Adam Smith

I am as funny as a clown
I am as thin as a stick
I am as fast as a cheetah
I am as big as a tree
I am as hard as a rock.
    I am just Adam!

Adam Smith (11)
Our Lady's Catholic Primary School

The Wind

The wind flings through the air,
Slowly stripping trees bare.
When the wind goes we'll celebrate,
Until then we'll have to wait.

The wind pushes our windowpane.
It also pushes the rain.
The wind blows our flowers,
With its awesome powers.

The wind takes our umbrellas,
It's like propellers.
Wind blows until it's white,
It mostly comes in the night.

The wind takes us away,
But we really want to stay.
Sometimes we want to play,
But the wind blows all day.

Alex Puddicombe (10)
Our Lady's Catholic Primary School

Oliver Twist

All children lined up with their gruel
With a wicked man who was very cruel
All children with sad faces
All going at very slow paces
Oliver said, 'Can I have some more?'
Mr Slout said, 'He was the greediest boy he'd ever saw.'
He took him to a man called Fagin
Oliver did not have to pay him
Oliver had a good time there
He thought that life was very fair.

Katie White (11)
Our Lady's Catholic Primary School

Tim's Bedroom

In Tim's bedroom there were:
Eight ants in a jam jar
Seven mice eating cornflakes
Six kittens under his bed
Five snakes behind his TV

> What shall we do?
> What shall we do?
> Tim's bedroom has turned into
> A zoo!

Four monkeys jumping around and all over the place
Three snow tigers on the end of his bed
Two fat bats in a dark dark corner
One elephant knocking at the door

> What shall we do?
> What shall we do?
> Tim's bedroom has turned into
> A zoo!

CJ Anderson (9)
Our Lady's Catholic Primary School

The Wind

The wind blows the world with his icy breath
He blows the clouds across the sky
And the trees bend at the sight
Of the wind crawling through their branches.

But when the winter says goodbye to the earth,
And the sun begins to shine hot and hard
The wind sends his soft breeze
To cool the land with his warm heart.

Beth Davies (11)
Our Lady's Catholic Primary School

The Hare And Tortoise

There once was a hare
That loved and loved to boast
There once was a tortoise
That loved to eat toast.

The hare wanted a race
To prove that he was fast
And prove that the tortoise
Would definitely be last.

'I want a race,' said the hare
So the race was set,
In the creepy woods
Where there were foxes that slept.

On the day
There was a big fuss
The hare was saying
'Tortoise you need to catch the bus.'

3, 2, 1, go!
Off went Hare, feet on fire,
His feet would
Have definitely burned like a tyre.

The hare went out of sight
And felt like a little sleep,
He slept all day
So the tortoise went by, not a peep.

The tortoise hobbled on
He went over the finish line
The hare woke up
From a sleep very fine.

'I win, I win.'
But the tortoise had finished already
'How, how did you win?'
'I took my time and I was steady.'

James McKeon (11)
Our Lady's Catholic Primary School

Holiday Memories

I journeyed into jungles
I swam the deepest sea
I climbed the highest mountain
And a monkey tree.

I visited the planets
I lit up all the stars
I chatted to a parrot
On its way to Mars.

I sailed across the ocean
I drove a greyhound bus
I rode across the desert
On a hippopotamus.

I chased a band of pirates
Completely round the bend
And now the summer's over
And this is the end.

Megan Duckworth (8)
Our Lady's Catholic Primary School

Snow

I drift, in silence, landing on my toes,
Melting icicles start dripping from my nose.
My cold icy fingers scraping down glass,
I throw my white carpet to cover the grass.

My eyes are like silver, they shine and twinkle,
My soft and smooth body, not even a wrinkle.
I look like a dancer, jumping and leaping
I lay, silent on the ground, whilst I'm sleeping.

When the sun shines on me, I run away
But when it's cold again, I'll come to play.

Jake Brown (10)
Our Lady's Catholic Primary School

Pigeons

Pigeons normally hang down town
But when they get kicked
They always frown.

My nickname is
Pigeon and guess what
I have a bird religion!

They always do their daily
Droppings and after that
They get a good whooping.

Their best friend is a tramp
And they use him for a camp.

Thank you for listening
To my birdie song
It will dwell in your memory
For long and long!

Alex McKeon (9)
Our Lady's Catholic Primary School

The Rain

The rain falls like a person from a bungee,
Wet and cold.
It falls in autumn
When the leaves drop.

People hide inside because of the rain,
On miserable days.
The rain shoots down like a bullet
From a gun.

When autumn ends,
The people are happy.

Jordan Rainford (11)
Our Lady's Catholic Primary School

Tom Cat

Tom cat's eyes are stars in the sky
His ears are tattered leaves
His teeth are little rose thorns
And his tail is a rolled up sleeve.

Tom cat's fur is like wire wool
His miaow is a warning sign
His claws are as sharp as razor blades
And his paws are like wet pads.

Tom cat's speed is like a lightning bolt
His springy paws help him pounce
Onto walls
His eyesight like a fox
His listening like a wild bear
Beware!

Ashleigh Kane (11)
Our Lady's Catholic Primary School

The Boy Who Ate The Bunny

There once was a little boy
He had a little toy
The toy said, 'Oi.'

The boy thought this was funny
So he bought a little bunny
And the bunny liked honey.

But only when it was sunny
So the boy ate the bunny
And the bunny was stuck in his tummy.

Timothy McGuinness (10)
Our Lady's Catholic Primary School

Joel's Bedroom

In Joel's bedroom there were:
Eight ants in a jam jar,
Seven mice eating cornflakes,
Six kittens eating tar,
Five mice eating rice,
What shall we do?
What shall we do?
Joel's bedroom has turned into a zoo!
Four monkeys swinging,
Three elephants stomping around,
Two lions roaring all night,
One penguin all alone,
What shall we do?
What shall we do?
Joel's bedroom has turned into a zoo.

Michael Bradbury (9)
Our Lady's Catholic Primary School

My Kitten

My kitten is sweet
My kitten is playful
My kitten is brilliant
My kitten is good
My kitten loves to eat
My kitten loves me
My kitten loves her toys
But where is my kitten?
My kitten loves to hide
She loves to hide under my bed.

Natalie Gethins (8)
Our Lady's Catholic Primary School

Colours

What is red?
The shed is red.

What is green?
The grass is green
With all the flowers
In between.

What is blue?
The sea is blue
With all the fish
Swimming deep.

What is yellow?
The sun is yellow
Shining brightly.

What is orange?
An orange is orange.

James Whibley (7)
Our Lady's Catholic Primary School

Smiles

Smiles are everything to everyone
Smiles are always real
Smiles make lots of difference
Smiles sometimes need to seal.

Smiles make people happy
Smiles can make people sad
Smiles are always chirpy
Smiles can make you go mad.

Smiles are very beautiful
Smiles are very kind
Smiles are always attractive
Smiles are always what you need
If you're in a sad kind of mind!

Fern Baxter (10)
Our Lady's Catholic Primary School

The Sound Collector

A stranger called this morning
Dressed all in black and grey
Put every sound into a bag
And carried them away.

The munching of the Branflakes
The smashing of the bowls
The tapping of the fingers
The sniffing of the moles

The miaowing of the cat
The popping of the toast
The flapping wings on the bat.

A stranger called this morning
He didn't leave his name
Left us only silence
Life will never be the same.

Nicole Rainford (9)
Our Lady's Catholic Primary School

The Man Who Stole Our House

The man who stole our house
He dressed in black and white
He woke me up in the middle of the night
You won't believe it but he gave me a fright
He seemed to be very tight
He's the man who stole our house last night.

He seemed to be stealing my kettle
It was the dearest of all metal
But all of a sudden I had my kettle back
The neighbours had caught him back to jail
You go he went to jail because he thought
He saw a mouse it's the man who stole our house.

Liam Edwards (10)
Our Lady's Catholic Primary School

What Is Black?

What is black?
The sky is black
When the stars are hidden.

What is yellow?
The dandelions are yellow
Swifting around the grass.

What is red?
A rose is red
Growing in the grass.

What is green?
A bush is green
Swifting in the wind.

Chloe McDermott (8)
Our Lady's Catholic Primary School

Seasons

Winter, summer, autumn and spring,

Snowy, boiling, rainy and windy,

All different kinds of seasons,

Which one is it now?

Winter is wonderful,
Summer is spectacular
Autumn is awesome,
Spring is super.

The birds sing in spring,
The sun comes out in summer,
The leaves fall in autumn,
The snow covers the ground in winter.

Kate Livesey (8)
Our Lady's Catholic Primary School

The Blinded Swordsman

He's taller
Than the biggest tree

He's stronger
Than a bull

He's more
Witty than a wild cat

He's as cunning
As a wolf

He's as talented
As an artist

He's as raging
As a T-rex

He's sharper
Than a knife

He's as destructive
As a bulldozer

He's quicker
Than a steed

Chorus
We know he cannot see us
But he knows we're there
He disposes of us quick
Then takes us to his lair.

He's as serious
As a jungle

He's as bitter
As salt

He's got more agility
Than a spider

He's as dangerous
As a volcano

He ignites
Quicker than fire

He's as fierce
As a lion

He's as
Terrifying as death

He's as murderous
As an axe

Chorus.

Nicholas Whibley (9)
Our Lady's Catholic Primary School

On Cold Winter Nights

On cold winter nights
It freezes and snows and
My hot water bottle
Toasts my toes.
On cold winter nights it is
Freezing cold, I snuggle up tight
And my teddy I hold.

Leah Hardman (8)
Our Lady's Catholic Primary School

Birthdays

Birthdays, birthdays, birthdays, are everywhere,
Everyday a year older than before.
Birthdays, birthdays, lots of presents,
Lots of money each birthday,
Birthdays, birthdays go to people's homes,
Lots of food to eat there.

Andrew McDermott (10)
Our Lady's Catholic Primary School

One Wet Whale

One wet whale
Two talking ticklish tigers
Three thinking things
Four flying falcons
Five fussy frogs
Six sensitive swans
Seven slithering snakes
Eight elephants eating eggs
Nine naughty newts
Ten tickly toads.

Antonia Swann (7)
Our Lady's Catholic Primary School

People

People are different colours like black,
Brown, yellow and beige.

People are rude and cheeky,
People are shy and outgoing.

People are different shapes and sizes,
People are fat and thin,
People are mean and nice.

Sadie McKeon (7)
Our Lady's Catholic Primary School

Imagine

Imagine a world without trees
Never seeing squirrels and birds playing
Never hearing leaves rustling and birds singing
No home for birds, squirrels or bats
No place for cats to play
No wood for desks at school or paper to work on.

Luke Verdon (11)
Our Lady's Catholic Primary School

A Zoo In My Room

In Olivia's bedroom there were:
Eight ants in a jam jar
Seven mice eating cornflakes
Six kittens in the cupboard
Five puppies under the quilt.

What shall we do?
What shall we do?
Olivia's bedroom
Has turned into a zoo!

Four monkeys hanging on the lampshade
Three hamsters running around like lunatics
Two rabbits under the pillow
One sparrow singing its tune making an awful din.

What shall we do?
What shall we do?
Olivia's bedroom
Has turned into a zoo!

Olivia Ward (10)
Our Lady's Catholic Primary School

Colours

What is blue?
The sea is blue
When it's full of fish.

What is yellow?
A sunflower is yellow
Swaying in the breeze.

What is green?
A leaf is green
Hanging from a vine.

Chase Anderson (7)
Our Lady's Catholic Primary School

Different Kinds Of Kids

Kids are big
Kids are small
Kids are fat
Kids are thin

Kids are hairy
Kids are normal
Kids are smelly
Kids are fresh

Kids are climbers
Kids are jumpers
Kids are sporty
Kids are lazy

Kids are playful
Kids are miserable
Kids are naughty
Kids are good.

Kids are cool
Kids are uncool
Kids are spotty
Kids are beautiful

Kids are strong
Kids are weak
Kids are handsome
Kids are horrible.

Nathan Stephenson (9)
Our Lady's Catholic Primary School

Barney

My old dog was called Barney
People think he is Barney the dinosaur
Barney is fluffier than a tiger
He is very playful and sweet.

Mathew Cameron (7)
Our Lady's Catholic Primary School

A Zoo In My Bedroom!

In Chris's bedroom there were:
Eight ants in a jam jar,
Seven mice eating cornflakes
Six kittens ripping up the bed
Five frogs jumping everywhere.

> What shall we do?
> What shall we do?
> Chris's bedroom
> Has turned into a zoo.

Four monkeys swinging from the roof
Three leeches sucking on my blood
Two elephants destroying my room
One lion eating the other animals.

> What shall we do?
> What shall we do?
> Chris's bedroom
> Has turned into a zoo.

Christien Galilee (10)
Our Lady's Catholic Primary School

One . . . Two . . . Three!

One worm wiggling
Two tiny toddles
Three thirsty things
Four frogs fat
Five fussy foxes
Six staring snakes
Seven silly singers
Eight elephants eating eggs
Nine naughty nuisances
Ten tired toddles.

Sophie Rutter (8)
Our Lady's Catholic Primary School

Mac Rain

Who is wet and cold
And knocks on the windowpane?
    Mac Rain!

Who is dull and grey
And sometimes falls on the plain?
    Mac Rain!

Who is a pain
And it never rains in Spain?
    Mac Rain!

Who runs down the lane
And falls down the drain?
    Mac Rain!

Who is runny and cold
And is a chain?
    Mac Rain!

Charlotte McCann (8)
Our Lady's Catholic Primary School

Mac Rain!

Who slows the trains and freezes your windowpanes?
Mac Rain!

Who rains on planes and pegs it down the lane?
Mac Rain!

Who often goes to Spain but clogs the drain?
Mac Rain!

Who really is a pain isn't that a shame?
Mac Rain!

Who makes the rain fall in a chain?
Mac Rain!

Myles Dennett (9)
Our Lady's Catholic Primary School

Mac Rain

Who is wet and cold
And the rain is a shame?
    Mac Rain.

Who is grey and freezing
And it runs through the lane?
    Mac Rain.

Who is glad and sad
Rain shooting on windows is a pain?
    Mac Rain.

Who is damp and soaked
And it falls on the pane?
    Mac Rain.

Who is dripping of water
And it goes down the drain?
    Mac Rain.

Emma Titcombe (9)
Our Lady's Catholic Primary School

The Big Chant

Hairy bugs, scary bugs,
Super duper fairy bugs.

Groovy bugs, movie bugs,
Round, long and tube bugs.

Jelly bugs, smelly bugs,
Crawling on your belly bugs.

Blue bugs, two bugs,
Really hard to chew bugs.

Toe bugs, show bugs,
Really hard to throw bugs.

Does this bug you?

Callum Wright (9)
Our Lady's Catholic Primary School

My Secret Friend!

My secret friend comes out and about
When the sun is shining in and out!

She's very quiet and very plain,
And she lives down our lane!

She's cool, she's cool, she's very cool
But she never comes in our swimming pool!

She doesn't like the rain or the dark
Or the night but she does like it when
The sun shines bright!

I've never heard her voice and I don't know her name
And she will never play a game!

But she's cool, she's cool, she's cool you know,
And this cool secret friend is my shadow!

Charlotte Williams (9)
Our Lady's Catholic Primary School

The Bug Chant

Hairy bugs, scary bugs,
Super duper fairy bugs.

Groovy bugs, movie bugs,
Round and hoovy bugs.

Jelly bugs, smelly bugs,
Crawling on your belly bugs.

Blue bugs, two bugs,
Really hard to chew bugs.

Toe bugs, snow bugs,
Really hard to throw bugs.

Jordan Kane (9)
Our Lady's Catholic Primary School

Mac Rain!

Who is wet and cold and
Knocks on the windowpane?
   Mac Rain!

Who is grey and mischievous
And thunders through the drain?
   Mac Rain!

Who comes down like a chain
And who is a big pain?
   Mac Rain!

Who is dripping wet and rolls
Down the lane?
   Mac Rain!

Niall Winn (8)
Our Lady's Catholic Primary School

About My Family!

My mum is kind,
Whatever I do she doesn't mind
She cleans the house and plays with my mouse
And that's my mum.

My dad is lazy and he's real crazy
He drinks a lot of beer
And has no fear
And that's my dad.

My brother is mean
He's in his teens
He gives me bruises
And he never loses
And that's my brother.

Rebecca Delooze (9)
Our Lady's Catholic Primary School

Food

Apples are juicy
Pears are ripe
Hot dogs are hot
Just like tonight.

Crisps are crispy
Biscuits are crunchy
Chocolate cake is smooth
But I like them chunky!

Oranges are orange
Peaches have stones
Pineapples are juicy
I have one at home.

Ice cream is cold
And very nice
Mushy peas
Are cold
And not at all
Nice!

Matthew Twiss (11)
Penketh Community Primary School

The Worm's War

Then his friend threw in the latest device
Phil went and got it, beyond all advice
His tail was split, his energy lost,
How many more will this dreaded war cost?

Then a new kind of disease tumbled down
If you didn't catch it you'd probably drown
So spare a thought for Phil and with it his friend
Who fought with honour and fought till the end.

So the worms battled on through hunger and pain
To fight a bit longer, just for victory again.

Christopher Venables (10)
Penketh Community Primary School

My Boyfriend

There is this boy in my class who I really fancy
He is really cool at school,
He has blonde hair and brown eyes
He is really sweet and funny,
He will eat anything he sees
It doesn't matter where it has been.

He has a little sister called Emily,
She is in my brother's class,
She really fancies him
But that is that,
So he has really funny friends
His names begins with M
And he has spider slippers
And all of his friends play with him.

Samantha Craven (11)
Penketh Community Primary School

Chocolate!

Chocolate sticks to your gum,
Chocolate tastes extremely *yum!*
It melts in the hot,
And I could eat a whole pot.
Chocolate sticks to your gum,
Chocolate tastes extremely *yum!*
If you eat loads you feel sick,
But don't feel sick, have another lick.
Chocolate sticks to your gum,
Chocolate tastes extremely *yum!*
There are different types of chocolate,
Mars, Crunchie and Snickers,
There are lots of other types,
But only some give you stickers.

Rachel Brownbill (11)
Penketh Community Primary School

Fear I Hate!

This fear I feel inside of me
I sit alone at night
Wondering what, how or who,
Gave me this terrible fright.

Is it a man or a woman,
Or is it just a dream?
I want to know now or never,
This fear I feel extreme.

I sense it coming nearer,
Please don't hurt me please
I can feel a shiver up my back
A storm is blowing the trees.

I am really glad it's over now,
No more fear and no more screams,
It is over now and is forever,
That horror dream I dreamed!

Amie Smith (11)
Penketh Community Primary School

Mountain

On a big mountain lives a sheep
Saw a ghost and went to sleep.
Woke up later on a donkey's back
So she jumped off his back and her legs went crack.
She went to the hospital in an ambulance
Now she's in a wheelchair and her wheels sound
Like a tank.
Later on she went home in her wheelchair that clanks
When she got home the donkey said, 'Bye'
Then there was a knock at the door with a
Mountain tiger delivering pie!

Emily Hedgcock (11)
Penketh Community Primary School

The Beach Of Tomorrow

I like the way the palm trees sway in the wind,
And the way they make the sound of crackling
Like when you click your fingers continually.

Also the way you can hear the peaceful and relaxing sea
When the tide comes in and out
Like a twirling tornado.

As well the golden sand sparkling in the sunlight
Like jewellery in a jewellery box.
As clean as can be.

And again also the way the hot dogs smell beautiful,
And at the hot dog stand it is extra warm
Like a sauna at an extremely hot temperature.
Then when you get out of that sauna-like hot dog stand
You will be as tanned as a brown buffalo.

Adam Rowles (11)
Penketh Community Primary School

Love?

Love is like you don't want to go to sleep,
Because reality is better than a dream!

Love is like your heart fluttering inside
So when you look up into the night sky
You imagine a dove!

Love is like an aching heart
It sometimes falls apart!

Look above
See a dove
Turn around
Guess what? . . . It's love!

Samantha Worrall (11)
Penketh Community Primary School

Dance

Little ballerina soft and sweet
Always light on her feet
Tiptoeing round the room
She will have a gorgeous groom
Little ballerina soft and sweet.

Little tap girl tap tap and step
Always dancing never stopping
Stamping round the room
She will get hit with a broom
Little tap girl tap tap and step.

Little modern dancer
Slide, slip and clap clap
Showing off in his show
Singing and dancing
My little modern dancer.

Little jazz dancer
Boogie, boogie get down tonight
Dancing to the saxophone
This jazz diver takes her place
Little jazz dancer.

Emily Stockton (10)
Penketh Community Primary School

Shopping!

Shopping, shopping, shopping, shopping,
Buy your designer clothes,
So good you will have the urge to pose.
You better take lots of cash
Everything else put in the trash,
Lots of money I lent her,
To go to the Trafford Centre,
Expensive is a word to describe it there
It makes people stop and stare.

Sophie Gamon (10)
Penketh Community Primary School

The Alien Train

I'm standing here at the station, with my dad
I'm very nearly five,
I'm holding his hand, extremely comfy and glad,
As I wait for our train to arrive.

Suddenly a gleaming, humungous, scarlet train steams
Into the station
Refreshing water from the tank is poured
I'm lost in a cloud of ice-white smoke,
As all the passengers climb aboard.

That's when I meet the alien,
He bowed his sea-blue, spotty head and muttered, 'Hi!'
He declares his name is Kalien
The journey starts and we shoot into the sky.

Where are we?
In space?
I distinguish planet Asperf
We're whizzing past stars at a tremendous pace
Slowly we turn and plunder back to Earth.

Eventually we get off the train
Out of the carriage that's shaped like a dome
'Don't worry!' I bellow. 'We'll come back again!'
We leap into the car and zoom back home.

Philippa Wheatley (11)
Penketh Community Primary School

The Zoo

A monkey is, so funky,
A snake is good to bake,
The bear always cares for the Mayor
Crocs rock when they eat a fox,
A deer has fear when hunters come near,
A bat likes to sleep on a mat!

Leanne Graham (11)
Penketh Community Primary School

My Car

Driving down the motorway
I wish that Honda would go away
Taking over so many drivers
Racing to beat the naughty skivers.
At 70mph through the desert,
Using every gear to upkeep my speed,
Dust gently floating in the air behind me,
I would also have to be careful,
Even though I'm alone there's still a
Chance of crashing.

Piece by piece
Building the dream,
Not giving up, no matter how hard.
On and on,
Finally she is built
I'll test her on the real roads of LA
Where she'll definitely pass the test
Even on the mean streets, she won't fail me.

My entire life I've dreamed about building my own car,
For years I thought having the fastest or fanciest car
Would bring me fame and glory,
But then I thought about building my own car.
A new model
Night and day I worked on the design of this car.

Jack Karran (11)
Penketh Community Primary School

How Unlucky Can you Get?

For breakfast I had scrambled egg
Me mum was in a mood and
Put it on me head.

On me way to school I was followed by a mutt
It bit me and I got a little cut.

Crossed the railroad got smashed by a train
Still alive in a lot of pain.

Just arrived at school
Been bullied, thrown in the pool.

We had a science test
Daydreaming didn't do the best
Had to do it again, enjoyed the rest.

Got blamed on Plaster of Paris
Sent to the Headmaster,
It was a disaster.

Got home, went to bed, turned on the lamp,
It gave me a nasty cramp.

I got to rest, I was shattered
Felt like I was dead.

I asked myself why am I alive?

Went to have a bath,
But went to sleep and drowned.

Alex Evans (11)
Penketh Community Primary School

Spirits!

The trees are rustling,
The snow is fluttering,
And the spirits are coming alive
But . . . when will they arrive?

The wolves are howling,
And the dogs are growling,
And the spirits are coming alive,
But . . . when will they arrive?

The ground is shaking,
And the trees are breaking,
The world's breaking in two
They're here now, what should I do?

The air is cold,
The cobwebs are old,
The spirits are out to get me,
How will I ever be free?

White figures creep slowly near
Something's increasing I think is my fear
My heart's in my mouth
Are the spirits moving south?

The light overhead is starting to flicker,
My heart is pounding quicker and quicker
The light has gone out
What should I do should I scream or shout?

Melissa Doan (11)
Penketh Community Primary School

Move Your Feet To The Beat

A week of dance
Get ready to prance
Come and watch
As it flies by.

Monday looming
Coming quick
Better go and tally
The hours till ballet.

Tuesday zooming
Coming quick
Foreign dances
In modern slick.

Wednesday coming
Coming quick
On the raz
So let's do jazz.

Thursday zooming
Coming quick
Must be tap
Because can't be rap.

Friday coming
Coming quick
Flamenco girls
Wear pearls.

Saturday's over
It will start again soon
Have a rest
Before Monday zooms.

Rebecca Casey (10)
Penketh Community Primary School

Murder In The Mansion

She crept up to the house
She was terrified although it was clear
It was like the air
Could sense her increasing fear.

She creaked open the door
And tiptoed inside
It was deserted and lonely
She could not hide.

Shivering shyly she crept
Into the small room
That place she could sense
Was her death tomb.

The poor girl had been lured there
As if she was bait
She was a distant spectator
Of her own doomed fate.

He was there too
Watching her, waiting to attack
But she knew there was something wrong
She got a shiver down her back.

He decided to do it then,
As gruesome as it seems,
He stabbed right through the middle
She let out a bloodcurdling scream.

Every time he sees that house
He remembers and it makes him care
That she never got a funeral
As nobody knew she was there.

Lucy Beech (11)
Penketh Community Primary School

An Unknown Storm

The rough, rough sea,
Is nastier than hot tea
It blows and throws and chucks and
Hurls everything at me.
It even tried the lighthouse with its
Gleaming shine of light.
The neighbours weren't impressed
With its continuous destructive bite.
It then knocked over a convoy ship
On an important flight.
We tried to take drastic measures to stop
Its evil bite
We didn't get any further and its reign
Is still on the run.
It swallowed everything in its path
Even a big hot bun.
Now it's heading for the Lake District
It's like it's got a gun.
We still have had no luck trying to catch this
Evil thing, I said while drinking some rum.

It has done enough damage said a bunch of singing men,
Now we take actions greater than were before
Once we got there we bombed the massive sea,
Once we noticed everything had cleared
We saw that we had just destroyed everywhere seen.
We shouldn't have gone to such lengths to destroy
Its evil reign
Now we know it was just an angry storm.

Alec Walker (11)
Penketh Community Primary School

A To Z Wild Animals

A is for antelope leaping and diving
B is for baboon eating bananas
C is for cheetah sprinting for prey
D is for dolphin swimming up and down
E is for elephant stomping the ground
F is for ferret soft and cute
G is for gorilla banging his chest
H is for hippo rolling in the water
I is for iguana prancing with joy
J is for Joey in its mum's pouch
K is for kangaroo looking for its Joey
L is for lion hunting for food
M is for monkey swinging in the treetops
N is for newts that run away
O is for octopus that squirts ink
P is for penguin that waddles on the coast
Q is for nothing, there's no animal there
R is for rat that scatters away
S is for snake that slithers around
T is for tortoise that's slow like a slug
U is for unicorn that's imagination
V is for venom that's extremely dangerous
W is for whale as big as a house
X is for nothing there's none out there
Y is for yack that sleeps all day
Z is for zebra with a lovely pattern.

Jessica McDonald (11)
Penketh Community Primary School

My Brother

This is my brother
He is like no other
He is the best
At being a pest
He takes after his mother.

Frank Richards (9)
Poulton Lancelyn Primary School

My New Bike

I have this new bike
Its colour is purple and blue
I say it's not for anyone
But only me and you.

It's good, it's bad
I really can't decide,
It's good, it's bad
It's really up to you.

My bike is really fast
It goes thirty miles an hour
It's the best bike in the world
Because it's got a lot of power.

It's good, it's bad
It's really up to you
It's good, it's bad,
I really can't decide.

It's bad because of my friends,
They think I'm a show off
I wish it wasn't so shiny
I wish, I wish, I wish.

Bethany Gerrard (7)
Poulton Lancelyn Primary School

The Rat

The lady comes down in her nighty
She asks the man for his ID
He checks for the beast under the stairs
It's left no trace except some hairs.

Oh where oh where can it be?
Is it a he or is it a she?
Left with no choice except to put some bait
Now all we have to do is wait.

Laura O'Meara (11)
Poulton Lancelyn Primary School

School, School And More School

I think some lessons in school are fun,
Especially ones that involve a drum,
But I would rather go to the pool,
Instead of acting like a fool.

I sometimes think lessons are boring
Especially ones with a lot of talking
I'd rather get straight on with my work,
Instead of acting like a jerk.

James McIver (9)
Poulton Lancelyn Primary School

The Silver Horse

Her silky mane glitters and gleams
Her soft, silver fur shines in the sun beams
The coloured ribbons tied on her tail
A gleaming, white smile will never fail
She gallops on off
When she has drunk from her trough
The silver horse
My silver horse.

Katie Hastings (9)
Poulton Lancelyn Primary School

Space Food

The sun is butter, to which you can spread on
The Earth's crust,
The moon is cheese, that has been scooped
From its pot called the Galaxy,
Pluto is a mini biscuit for afters,
Wash it down with Mars' red juice,
Served on top of Jupiter's plate.

Laura Armand (11)
Poulton Lancelyn Primary School

My Hound

I had a hound
But it went to the pound
I don't know why
But it ate a pie.
My dad got me another hound
But it soon went to the pound.
Then my nan had a bad back
Then my mum got me a rain mac
Soon I got a new cat
But it started to play with my hat.
But then it ate my pet rat
Then I got a new mat.
I loved my hound
But it went to the pound
I don't know why
But it ate a pie.

Lorna Hayden (8)
Poulton Lancelyn Primary School

The Book

One day I went to my mum,
And asked her for a book.
She said, 'Go to the library,
And have a good look.'

When I got to the library
I saw it on a shelf,
I picked it up and began to read
But it began to melt!

The library fined me £50
But I don't really care
'Anyway,' said my mum,
'It's the cost of your brother's underwear.'

Dulcie Wilkinson (9)
Poulton Lancelyn Primary School

My Dog Poppy!

My dog Poppy is as white as a snowflake,
With her little brown eyes,
Big bushy tail
And button black nose!

She loves running on the beach
And playing in the sea
Then when she is tired,
She enjoys the sleep!

My dog Poppy hates having a bath,
But then afterwards she enjoys
Sitting by the fire and being brushed!

But then at night when it's time for bed
She barks for a biscuit
And goes off into her own little land!

Emma Maddocks (11)
Poulton Lancelyn Primary School

The Horse With Goodness

When the horse comes out
Everyone stops
And stares
For every time she comes
She is as scruffy as a rat in a bin
But at home
When she is on her own
She turns into a unicorn!
With her mane and tail
As soft as silk
And a beautiful groomed body
She rides through the air
Invisible
And sends goodness to the world.

Ruth Buddle (9)
Poulton Lancelyn Primary School

Life

Life is beautiful
Life is excellent to me
Life is life
Life is breath
Life is excellent to me
You need life to be life
Life is your heart
Life is life for me
I need life to have life
Life is all I need.

Scott Richardson (9)
Poulton Lancelyn Primary School

Nightmares

In each house while everyone's asleep,
Slowly and steadily the grim reapers creep
And when it finally comes to dawn,
The leader of the reapers blows his horn.
Quietly they trudge back to their land,
With a scythe or a knife in each hand,
Gradually back to their land they creep,
While everyone else is fast asleep.

Lewis Evans (11)
Poulton Lancelyn Primary School

I Wish

I wish I had a pony
Which I could ride all night
I could fly it in the showering of the moonlight
Then suddenly a goblin came and gave me such a fright
But me and my pony galloped off into the night.

Quietly we went fast asleep
And that was the end of that goblin freak.

Melissa Noble (8)
Poulton Lancelyn Primary School

Summer Camp

Mum and Dad are sending me to summer camp
Whoopee
They thought it would be good for a weakling like me

To learn new skills and have some fun!
Will Mum and Dad miss their only son?

On the bus I'll soon be there
Looking forward to games, friends and fresh air.

First activity, rowing on the lake
There's a hole in the boat for goodness sake!

Second activity learning to tie knots
I can't believe I forgot the lot!

Singing songs in the pouring rain
Hope I don't have to come here again!

Weekend's over I'm on my way home
Never again will I moan about home.

Aaron Smith (10)
Poulton Lancelyn Primary School

Snowy

Snowy is my favourite horse
She likes to ride on her course
Her fur glitters in the sun
I like her because she is fun
In my dreams I see her dancing
Sometimes she is prancing
When I wake up in the morning
I look outside and think she's yawning
Snowy is my favourite horse
She likes to ride on her course.

Natalie Carpenter (9)
Poulton Lancelyn Primary School

I Dance

I dance in the morning,
I dance at night,
I want to dance
From the moment it's light.

I dance inside
I dance outdoors
I go to class
And I dance some more.

Dance makes me happy
Dance makes me smile,
Dance takes me somewhere else
For a while.

I've been dancing since I was two,
If I didn't dance, what else would I do?
Dancing to me is everything
If I didn't dance then maybe I'd
. . . Sing.

Emilie Sutcliffe (9)
Poulton Lancelyn Primary School

The Lion

I see a lion,
Looking at me,
With his eyes as brown as chocolate,
His shaggy brown mane shines in the sun,
He is now constantly staring at me.

He's now slowly moving,
While licking his fur.
He quietly crawls through the grass
Suddenly he strikes and catches his prey!
I think this lion is having a happy day.

Matthew Dobson (9)
Poulton Lancelyn Primary School

Hello My Name Is Pirate Sam

Hello my name is Pirate Sam,
And me I am a fool
The reason that I could not spell
When I went to school.

I had some sweets in my pocket,
Deep down inside my coat
Loads of sweets there were
They came round and round on a little float.

I had a musical teacher
We had a big bite
She had a big fat tummy
And got in a real fight.

She had a dog,
Who really stank
It had a weird tummy
And had a blank.

Natalie Fields (9)
Poulton Lancelyn Primary School

The Park

I'm glad that I live by the park
Because I know that after dark,
The park lights up without a fright,
The dandelions are the light.

But in the morning the lights are gone,
Because their work they have done,
I know they will come back tonight
The dandelions with their light.

I go to bed and there they are
I see them sitting there in the park,
Now I want to go and play
I'll have to wait till another day.

Fern Gordon (10)
Poulton Lancelyn Primary School

All The Little Animals

All the little animals from the snail to the fox
You may find them in meadows
For example take the fox.
With its big bushy tail and tiny paws,
With tufts between its ears and its powerful jaws.
But now we have the rabbit cuddly and round,
Its whiskers twitch as it bounces on the ground.
But don't forget the butterfly with its brightly coloured wings,
They wave and flutter gently in the wind.

Abigail Elias (9)
Poulton Lancelyn Primary School

Animals Galore

Animals, animals, animals, galore!
Animals' skins and so much more,
Go to the zoo and you will find,
Oh my goodness, a tiger that's kind!

Animals, animals, animals galore!
Animal paws and so much more,
Go to the zoo and you will find,
Oh my goodness, a zebra with a wonderful mind.

Katie McIver (9)
Poulton Lancelyn Primary School

Joe Rack

Joe Rack swang on a lamp post,
He likes to do it eating toast,
But one day when he was swinging around
He fell off and hit the tarmac ground,
As he was waving at Mr Morner
A car came flying around the corner,
It gave him a knock on the head,
Next day in hospital he was . . . dead!

Jamie Morris (8)
Poulton Lancelyn Primary School

Wounds Of War

The soldier creeps silently ahead,
But the sun has failed and the moon is dead.
Shadows move across his face
The others gone without a trace.
Does he know he's the only one?
Does he know his hopes have gone?

As he hears the guns of war,
He honestly asks, 'Is there any more?'
Now the clouds of lightning and thunder
Circle the skies of the evening plunder
He heard a cease, he put on a frown,
He knew the enemy were coming down.
Clenching his gun with sweaty hands,
His heart was beating like twenty bands.

The footsteps stopped, a gun was fired,
He clenched his stomach, his guts got wired,
He fell to his knees and then to the floor,
'No,' he said, 'there is no more.'

As he gets to Heaven
To St Peter he will plead,
'To defeat my attacker, I had to do,
But for war, there was no need.'

Abhijith Thippeswamy (11)
Poulton Lancelyn Primary School

The Tiger

A tiger is like
A sly evil falcon
With a swishing, stripy tail
And black beady eyes.

Pouncing quickly on its prey
In the sunlight or moonlight
A tiger is always hungry.

Zoë Brunton (9)
Poulton Lancelyn Primary School

Pet War

Sergeant Fluffy sends out his troops
As Corporal Rover sorts out his groups,
Scratches and kicks,
Barking and hiss,
And the hurricane budgies swoop.

Lieutenant Muffin gives out his order
Private Rex crosses the borders,
As the cats growl
Before the dogs howl,
The eagles send forth their marauders.

Battle ends on that horrible day
Those involved had a price to pay.
Nicks, neck bites,
Cuts and parasites,
So all of this for a nap on the hay.

Joe Cullen (10)
Poulton Lancelyn Primary School

Empty

Your hutch is now empty,
But my eyes are full,
Of tears I don't want to be there.

Whether you're here,
Or whether you're not,
In my heart you will always be near.

I am missing you loads,
It's only a day,
Since I found you had passed away.

But just so you know,
I'll never forget,
That you were the best ever pet.

Lauren Price (10)
Poulton Lancelyn Primary School

Girls Rule

Girls rule
Boys drool
Girls are pretty
Boys are gitty
Girls are the best
Boys are pests.

So now you see
Girls like me
Are the best.

Louise Jones (8)
Poulton Lancelyn Primary School

Cheetah

There you creep in the tall dancing reeds
Your slit emerald green eyes carefully following your prey
And there you pounce
Sprinting like the Michael Schumacher of all animals
Your spots become smudges
Your fine, smooth fur glistens in the morning sunlight
You sink your blade like teeth into your prey
A roar of victory as you return to the dancing reeds.

Molly Dyas (10)
Poulton Lancelyn Primary School

The Day

I know this will be a happy day
'Cause all I do is sing and play.

Throw a stick, make it stand
They are like a marching band.

But when I go to bed I'm sad
Because I miss all the fun I've had.

Rachel Winstanley (9)
Poulton Lancelyn Primary School

Shops

Down at the shops
I met a man called Fred
Fred said, 'So I want some money
To buy a loaf of bread.'

Matthew Hicks (7)
Queens Road Primary School

The Cloud

As I watch the rain and thunder pass by
Then it stops and it goes really far away
And we can go out to play.
It is nice playing out in my garden
Then I go and have my tea
And the black clouds up in the sky
Have just begun to cry.

Gabrielle Flude (7)
St Margaret Mary's Junior School, Liverpool

Weather Fight

The sun is out; it's come to play,
Out comes the rain and spoils the day
The rain soaks us and our friends, all we want is our great sun
Sun, sun please come back, and fight the rain
You will win, you're so good.
Bam, bash! Come on, come on let's see who won
The sun! Oh no here is the wind, wind wind go away
Hip hip, hooray, hip hip hooray!

Lewis Joinson (9)
St Mary's CE Primary School, Wirral

My Kitten

When I wake up in the morning
I see my kitten snoring
When my kitten awakes
He drinks out of a cup
In the afternoon
He plays with a cocoon
For her lunch
Well she had brunch
Then it came to night
And I said sleep tight.

Amy Edwards (9)
St Mary's CE Primary School, Wirral

Weather Poem

When we were on holiday it was spitting madly
Then you see the sun it was shining sadly
Then the hurricane was turning badly
Next the hail smashing down
Then the thunder bashing down
Then there was not a sound in the quiet moonlight.

Eleanor Caitlin Chambers (9)
St Mary's CE Primary School, Wirral

The Weather

I got soaking wet
When I was walking home
Then it started to snow
And I was dancing in the snow
Until night-time came
I saw a cloud again.

Kelsie Oldfield (8)
St Mary's CE Primary School, Wirral

Wacky Weather

Hurricanes can make you mad
Rain can make you very sad
If you want some fun
Please wait for the sun
Thunder can give you a fright
Sometimes it comes with a flash of light
In the winter falling snowflakes
Will freeze the water in the lakes
A storm can bring a flood
There will be lots of mud
In the spring the leafy trees
Wave their branches in the gentle breeze.

Tom Davies (8)
St Mary's CE Primary School, Wirral

Spain

Last night it was black!
When we arrived in Spain
Today it was raining so we went outside
But I saw a really big rainbow

So we took off our raincoats and put them inside
The hotel room
But it started to rain *again!*

Heather Hillbeck (8)
St Mary's CE Primary School, Wirral

Holiday Memories

Weather dripping aggressively and I was soaked to the skin
The weather was really hot and I was sweating to the brim
The next day it was freezing cold I had icicles on my chin
                                        and frostbite on my feet.
The next day we were boogying to the beat
They are some holiday memories.

Sarah Edwards (7)
St Mary's CE Primary School, Wirral

Raining And Thundering

The sky went dark and the clouds went from light to night
When a strike of lightning shattered the bins
The rain came down lightly at first
Then harder and harder
It rained on the street,
The water rose up to the step and into the door,
Up to the windows in the living room
Up the stairs and into my room
All of a sudden the rain stopped,
A man swam to the grid,
Opened it, letting all the water flow away.

William Foster (8)
St Mary's CE Primary School, Wirral

Holiday Madness With Weather Problems

We're all going on a summer holiday and it will be hot
But very full on the plane.

But it might rain
There's more chance of it being a sunny day
It may be cloudy or snowing who knows?
Definitely not me!
The weather isn't up to me,
It makes its own mind up
So don't ask me for the weather.

Connor Barry (9)
St Mary's CE Primary School, Wirral

The Black Tornado

The black, loud tornado swept across Britain
        making the sky go dark and the sea rise,
Flooding the streets of Britain.
Everyone shut their doors and windows so water
                        never got into their houses.

Conor Hallwood (7)
St Mary's CE Primary School, Wirral

At Home

I am roasting hot
Today it is freezing cold
I was playing out in the sun
It was raining outside
I was crying inside
I was fed up.

Daniel Reece (7)
St Mary's CE Primary School, Wirral

Holiday Memories

When I arrived it was raining all the time
I was freezing, and then there were hailstones
On the last night was thunder and lightning
We got home and it was boiling.

Jessica Nevitt (8)
St Mary's CE Primary School, Wirral

Snow

Snow
Soft, fluffy,
Smooth, frosty, white,
You can make snowmen,
Snow.

Winter
Winter,
Cold, raining
Windy, snowy, icy
We can't go outside,
Winter.

Charlotte Smith (9)
St Pauls RC Primary School, Blackburn

Snow/Ice

Snow
Cold, icy
Chilly, frosty, crunchy
Fun to fight in the snow.

Ice
Frosty, transparent
Icy, fresh, crystal
You can ice skate on ice.

Jade Duxbury (8)
St Pauls RC Primary School, Blackburn

Sunflower Is Like A Baby

A baby is delicate and soft like the petals of the sunflower
A baby is tiny and has a long way to grow like a sunflower
A baby is wonderful and brightens up your life like a sunflower
A baby is sensitive and fragile like a sunflower
A baby will turn its head to the sun like a sunflower.

Charlotte Hindle (9)
St Pauls RC Primary School, Blackburn

Snow

Snow is like a blanket on the ground.
Snow drops down like dancing feathers from the sky.
Snow is like freezing cold ice cubes.
Snow is crisp and clean and glistens like diamonds.
Snow is fun when you make snowmen.
I love snow.

Nicole Cassidy (9)
St Pauls RC Primary School, Blackburn

Winter

W hirling, twirling, winding winds,
  I cicles hanging like sharp, shiny knives
  N estled animals all snug in their beds
  T alking to neighbours will not happen now,
  E veryone making snowmen with soft, fluffy snow
  R iding sledges at tremendous speed down hill.

Katrina Tomlinson (8)
St Pauls RC Primary School, Blackburn

What Is Red?

What is red? A traffic light is red they go on and off
What is black? A Ferrari is black they go fast
What is silver? Window frames are silver. They hold windows in
What is yellow? Chips are yellow you eat them
What is gold? Pants are gold you wear them
What is green? Trees are green they grow.

Ben Hanley (7)
St Teresa's RC Primary School, Irlam

What Is Red?

What is red? Rudolf's nose is red,
Who helps Santa to get to the children.
What is black? Gorillas are black.
They *bang* with their hands on their chests.
What is silver? Tin foil is silver it is shiny and scrunchy.
What is yellow? Chips are yellow
You eat them and they are crunchy.
What is white? A mouse is white
Scuttling through the night.
What is blue? The sky is blue travelling through.

Joseph Denneny (7)
St Teresa's RC Primary School, Irlam

What Is Red?

What is red? A postbox is red
You post letters through it.

What is black? The dark is black
You can't see in the dark.

What is silver? Some metal is silver
You can make things with it.

What is yellow? A banana is yellow
You eat them and they are creamy.

What is green? A crocodile is green
It eats people.

What is white? Some wax is white
Like I've got on my hair.

Alex Lightfoot (7)
St Teresa's RC Primary School, Irlam

What Is Red?

What is red? The devil is red
Red all over
What is black? The middle of your eye is black
Very very black
What is silver? A disco ball is silver
Sparkling away.
What is yellow? A banana is yellow.
Yellow matches the name.
What is white? Wax is white
Very white.
What is blue? Manchester City football top
Blue, blue very blue
What is grey? A dolphin is grey
Swishing through the water.

Lewis Holland (7)
St Teresa's RC Primary School, Irlam

What Is Red?

What is red? United's shirt is red,
Simply the best.
What is black? A witch's hat is black
She wears it all the time.
What is silver? Jewellery is silver,
Shiny and sparkly.
What is yellow? Pyramids are yellow
Pyramids are big.

Christopher Davenport (7)
St Teresa's RC Primary School, Irlam

What Is Red?

What is red? Lips are red nice and shiny.
What is black? Mud is black all squelchy.
What is silver? Pots and pans are silver really noisy.
What is yellow? Banana is yellow nice and tasty
What is orange? An orange is orange round and round.
What is blue? The sea is blue that makes a beautiful sound
What is green? Grapes are green really juicy.

Georgia Burbidge (7)
St Teresa's RC Primary School, Irlam

What Is Red?

What is red? Postbox is red you put your letters in.
What is black? A gorilla is black up in the trees.
What is silver? Silver is silver shiny and sparkly.
What is yellow? A melon is yellow, juicy as can be.
What is grey? An elephant is grey spraying water out.
What is pink? A pig is pink splashing in the mud.

Kieran Farrell (7)
St Teresa's RC Primary School, Irlam

What Is Red?

What is red? Homework books are red, we do our homework in them.
What is black? Manchester United kits are black they play hard.
What is silver? A coin is silver we pay with coins.
What is yellow? A daisy is yellow they are beautiful and soft.
What is white? A swan is white furry with an orange beak.

Alex Nelson (7)
St Teresa's RC Primary School, Irlam

Harry Potter

As thunder strikes
Voldemort appears

There is no relaxing
When you're at war with Voldemort.

You will end up in Heaven
Unlike *Harry Potter.*

They might be enemies
But *Harry* will 'always' win!

I know *he* will!
I know *he* will!

Harry Potter is no girl
He fights like a man

Harry is triumphant
He defeated Lord Voldemort

Voldemort gave him a scar
But Harry stays calm!

Sirius is amazed
He looks after Harry.

Harry feels like he's flying on a Hipogriff
Over the moon.

Lewis Horrocks (11) & Polly Pattinson (10)
St Peter's CE Primary School, Wirral

Winnie The Pooh

Winnie the Pooh
Lives in the Hundred Acre Wood,
Loves his honey
Tastes so good.

Piglet, Tigger and Eeyore
Are his main best friends,
They always stay together
And their friendship never ends.

Tigger entertain's them.
Bouncing here and there
Winnie, Piglet and Eeyore
Just stand and mile and stare.

Winnie the Pooh is soft cuddly and small,
He is my favourite bear of them all.

Bethany Gillen (9)
St Peter's CE Primary School, Wirral

The Sea

The sea is rumbling
The sea is rough,
The sea is tumbling,
The sea is tough,
It crashes and crumbles
Against the rocks.

The sea is sparkling,
The sea is still,
The sea is salty,
It gives a chill.
It smoothly rustles
Upon the sand.

Look out there's a tidal wave!

Nicholas Jones (9)
St Peter's CE Primary School, Wirral

Leopard Was Created

Leopard began.
For his eyes
He stoke the deepness of a canyon
He seized the silence of a cave
He snatched the greenness of the forest
And his cold eyes were made.

He grabbed the curve of the moon
He took the stealth from an adder
He stole the sharpness of a spear
And his paws were formed.

For his coat
He took the softness from velvet
He seized the brightness of the sun
He took the darkness from the night,
And leopard was born.

Edward Gibbs (10)
St Peter's CE Primary School, Wirral

The Sea

I like the sea
The sparkling sea
The crashing rough sea.

Some days it is really choppy,
But that doesn't stop me.

I like the sea,
The rushing, roaring sea,
I like it when it is still and calm,
That's when it really sparkles.

Katherine Astbury (7)
St Peter's CE Primary School, Wirral

To Be Afraid

I'm afraid of lots of things,
Nobody knows what fear brings,
I become rigid and meet the mouse of fear,
Nobody knows can't you hear?

Spiders jumping from ledge to ledge,
Scorpions creeping on me from a hedge,
Fearful barking from nowhere,
When I'm set on a terrible dare.

Woodlice in my bed at night,
I become shivery at just the sight,
Snakes slithering like a mouse
I just want to go back to my house.

These are some things I am scared of,
My lungs twist and I start to cough,
I turn to ice and a hot oven,
And then I become all woven!

Emily Yates (9)
St Peter's CE Primary School, Wirral

Fear

I'm really scared of war,
It shivers at my door,
It hisses out loud,
And gathers like a cloud.

War is not good
It causes spilling of blood,
It shouts out *fear*,
And destroys all that's dear.

The bullets and booms echo in my head,
I pray for the people shot down dead,
What if war comes when I'm a man?
Should I fight if I can?

Harry Twells (10)
St Peter's CE Primary School, Wirral

The Magic Box
(Based on 'Magic Box' by Kit Wright)

I will put in my box . . .
The shine from a diamond, polished and cleaned,
The delicate touch of a newborn baby,
The gentle sound of a purring kitten.

I will put in my box . . .
The crashing sound of thunder,
The sharp sting of a nettle leaf,
The doom and death of a skeleton.

I will put in my box . . .
The light and dark of day and night,
The blue and green of the Earth,
All the sounds of the animals.

I will put in my box . . .
The sight of a venomous snake,
The streak of sunlight from a glowing star,
The smoothness of a blade of grass.

My box is fashioned from clouds and dreams
And patterned with leaves and berries.
Its hinges are the brown knuckles of goblins' fingers.
I will fly in my box from mountaintop to mountaintop
In the empty hills of everywhere.

Jessica Rushworth (9)
St Peter's CE Primary School, Wirral

Being Afraid

When I'm afraid I shiver with fear.
The dark is like a lion biting me.
The ghosts are howling with terror and panic.
When I'm afraid I blink and clutch my heart.
When I'm afraid I try and conquer my fear by lighting the sky.
I am OK but I still can be afraid.

Natalie Lowry (9)
St Peter's CE Primary School, Wirral

My Heart Lies In Glasgow

I will arise and depart now,
North, to Glasgow town,
The urban city centre,
New and old mingle alike,
Fine architecture of buildings,
I shall walk in many great houses,
And lie in my poster bed.

I shall visit the city Hubbub,
The bustle of the main street,
The brilliant sun arising over the Clyde,
To where the many races gather
The rays of the blue sky glistening,
In the water
Which laps at the pier.

I shall arise and depart now,
And stay there for years more,
Alas this is where my heart lies,
But yet I sit in my dull classroom,
Dreaming of where my heart lies,
I am sleeping I don't care,
I follow my heart.

Alasdair Cunningham (10)
St Peter's CE Primary School, Wirral

As The Year Goes On

Butterflies flutter in the summer sun
Birds are singing mornings begun,
The colour of the sky as it turns to dawn
The feel of the dew on the frozen lawn,
The big silver birch with falling leaves
The huge grey spider begins to weave,
The wood is burning on the evening fire
All these things I desire!

Lily Taylor (11)
St Peter's CE Primary School, Wirral

The Magic Box
(Based on 'Magic Box' by Kit Wright)

I will put in my box . . .
The last glimpse of the Earth
The delicate colours of the galaxy
The shine of a rainbow's end.

I will put in my box . . .
The smile of the sun and the frown of the moon.
Life itself and death too
And the fresh air of a new morning.

I will put in my box . . .
The past and future so everyone can see what was before
The Seven Wonders of the World
And the scales from the rainbow fish.

I will put in my box . . .
The refreshing soil of all the planets
The echo of the water and air.

My box is fashioned from
The generous spirits of the generation that onced lived.
My box is guarded by the voices of the Gods
Its hinges are formed by a dragon's leg joint.
I shall explore the mysterious dangers of the world.
And I shall learn new skills.

Alistair Jones (11)
St Peter's CE Primary School, Wirral

Spiders

Big spider crawling slowly
Little spider scuttling quickly
Scary spider creeping hastily
Mean spider scattering rapidly
Hairy spider jumping briskly
Bald spider menacingly motionless
Jumping spider leaping sneakily.

Ben Robinson (10)
St Peter's CE Primary School, Wirral

The Magic Box
(Based on 'Magic Box' by Kit Wright)

I will put in my box . . .
The sparkling shine of a red ruby,
The natural colours of the rainbow,
And the song of the dawn chorus.

I will put in my box . . .
The revs of a dirt bike,
The sound of a bike skidding
The sound of birds tweeting in a tree.

My box is fashioned with thunder and ice,
Embroidered with the bright sunshine,
Its hinges are formed by bees' knees.
I shall stand on the pyramid of Giza
And then glide into the soft hot and smooth sand.

Joe Clarke (9)
St Peter's CE Primary School, Wirral

Mouse Began

She stole the grey of the sky
She took the brown of the soil
To make her coat.

For her claws,
She seized the sharpness of an icicle
And the smallness of a pea.

Mouse stole the blackness of a bead,
And snatched a light,
For her eyes.

Mouse grabbed the thinness of a fishing wire,
She pinched an unravelled ball of grey string
For her whiskers.

Elle Lawrenson (11)
St Peter's CE Primary School, Wirral

Spiders!

Spiders are terrifying
Huge and fast
Out of all my favourites insects,
They would come last!

They make me feel like jelly
Wobbling on a plate,
When one is right in front of me,
I just cannot think straight!

A jelly's free to wobble,
Just like shivery me.
The only difference is that
You can't eat me for tea!

A little mouse of fear
Scuttles up my spine,
All my hairs stick up on end
They don't look like mine!

It only takes a little push
And I will start to break,
But then Mum comes to rescue me
And gives me a great big shake!

Sophie Kellner (9)
St Peter's CE Primary School, Wirral

The Rat Rap

The rapping rat lives down a hole,
Yo, yo, yo, yo!

I take my time by eating cheese
But I speed up when I am eating fleas

I'm the best at throwing all the dirt,
All over my mum's pretty skirt!

I get my friends and call them Bert,
- Shout rapping rat *super dirt!*

Zoe Turner (10)
St Peter's CE Primary School, Wirral

Being Scared

I am scared of a lot of things
Dogs who bite,
Dark in the night.
When I get lost,
When I get bossed.
When a spider comes near me,
When I spill very hot tea.
When I see posters of dinosaurs,
I have to stare and I pause.
All these things aren't very nice,
So when I look at them I turn to ice.
When I am scared I feel myself shiver,
My heart beats fast,
My lips quiver.

Hannah Dowler (10)
St Peter's CE Primary School, Wirral

I Want A Pet

A dog
A hog,
A cat called Mog,
That's all I want,
I asked my mum
'No'
I asked my dad
'No'
Will I ever get?
A dog,
A hog,
And a cat called Mog
'No!'

Claire Murray (10)
St Peter's CE Primary School, Wirral

The Sea

Calm then still,
Sparkling then blowing,
Lashing then flashing,
Storming and performing.

Grumpy to angry,
As it lashes and crashes,
Against the slippery rocks,
On the sandy shore.

Sand and dust blown in to the sea,
Then crushed into smithereens
As it surrounds the lighthouse.

It sneaks round the door,
It creeps up the steps,
Turning every brick
Into big lumps of sand.

Pulling shells, rocks, sand
And dust with it.
It flows up and down
The steps like a mirror.

Aidan Mould (8)
St Peter's CE Primary School, Wirral

Pat The Cat

The groovy cat crawled down the alley
Pat the cat and dancing Sally

I'm Pat the cat how do you do
I scratch my claws on top of you.

Miaow

I'm the best at the wicked hip
I'm number one at doing a flip

All you cats who wear a patch
Shout Pat the cat - super scratch!

Amanda Trenholm & Zoe Williamson (11)
St Peter's CE Primary School, Wirral

Chocolate . . .

It lies on the table in temptations hours,
Dark chocolate, milk chocolate, or white which is the best?
Oh come mighty chocolate give me your power,
Milk chocolate is the best it reigns o'er the rest.
The master of chocolate sits upon this throne,
His dog is standing there looking at me,
The dog whining over a juicy bone.
Chocolate covered crispies waiting for me,
Milky Way is ok but the Galaxy beats it,
It stops you from being in a bad mood,
Galaxy rules over the chocs even the Indians eat it,
Chocolate is the best of all the foods,
Crunchie, Fudge and Chomp are different makes,
I'd rather hold chocolate than a big angry snake!

Laura Dawson & Sarah Rothwell (11)
St Peter's CE Primary School, Wirral

Snow

The white snow came down at quarter past two.
We've been waiting for this day for over a year,
The wind made everyone turn shades of blue,
Happy as can be are the children now snow is here,
It covered the ground like a white bed sheet,
We couldn't tell if it was hail or snow,
No one in town went out in their bare feet,
Everyone started to say ho, ho, ho.
On top of the pool was a carpet of ice,
You could see the birds snuggled in their nest,
In front of the fire were the little mice.
All of the children wore woolly jumpers over their vest.
They got into their PJ's and went up to bed
And they had sweet dreams with their little fluffy ted.

Kate Hill (11)
St Peter's CE Primary School, Wirral

I Am The Wind

I am the wind,
I am the wind,
Swirling, whirling,
I am the wind.

I am the wind,
I am the wind,
Bullying the daffodils,
I am the wind.

I am the wind
I am the wind,
Strong and almighty
I am the wind.

I am the breeze,
I am the breeze,
Swaying lightly,
Dying, down,
Dying, down,
Dying,
Dying,
Still.

Natasha Doyle (11)
St Peter's CE Primary School, Wirral

Burtle The Turtle - Super DJ

Burtle the turtle does DJ
He never wears no PJ's

Yoyo Burtle does no jazz
He does not even use dazz.

Burtle the turtle knows all the moves.
He is just learning the groves.

And all you turtles shout: *DJ Burtle*

Alex Hazlehurst (9)
St Peter's CE Primary School, Wirral

The Magic Box
(Based on 'Magic Box' by Kit Wright)

I will put in my box . . .
The greatness of Everton
And the blinding shine of the sunlight
Like the sound of a tank raging down a hill.

I will put in my box . . .
The golden gleam of a winning cup.
The sparkling water at night.
The speed of an African elephant.

My box is fashioned by the blood of a spider
The hinges are made of skin
I shall stand on the highest building and fall to a cushiony bed
And wake by the smell of baking biscuits.

Josh Beck (11)
St Peter's CE Primary School, Wirral

The Magic Box
(Based on 'Magic Box' by Kit Wright)

I will put in my box . . .
The sparkle of a star in the silver sky,
The beautiful pattern of a butterfly's wing,
The tranquil tears of a mother's love.

I will put in my box . . .
The precious purr of a perfect feline
The smoothest skin of a turquoise dolphin,
The aggressive roar of the most ferocious lion.

My box is fashioned from fire and ice,
Embroidered with the softest snow,
The hinges are made from the brightest light.

Nicole Page (9)
St Peter's CE Primary School, Wirral

Magic Box
(Based on 'Magic Box' by Kit Wright)

I will put in the box . . .
A blue flamed coal fire
Milk breathing dragon and a fire-breathing cow.

I will put in the box . . .
A horrifying hound howling at the dead of night
The sound of a baby approaching its first cry
The loudness of an elephant leaping from tree to tree.

I will put in the box . . .
The neatness of an artistic drawer
The carefulness of a specialist doctor and
The perfectness of a musician.

I will put in the box . . .
A television with no colour
A radio with no sound and
A human with no voice.

My box is designed with
Smiles and loveable happiness
And wishes squashed at the very bottom
With a golden sugar lock.

I shall gallop with my golden horse in my box
Up the storm breaking whirling waterfall
And leap off the rocks to the still warm beach.

Amy Williams (11)
St Peter's CE Primary School, Wirral

Spain

I will arise and go now to the warmth of Spain
Sunbathing next to the pool watching the children play.

I would dwell there in the place I love most,
Staying in a first class hotel with endless amounts of food.

My heart lies there but not my body,
I'm in the classroom all cold with blackboards surrounding me.

Emily Clarke (9)
St Peter's CE Primary School, Wirral

Summer Holidays

Summer holidays soaking up the sun
Say goodbye to the winter and the cold,
A way to describe the summer is 'fun!'
Seeing all my friends which are new and old
On holiday I'm sitting in the pool,
It seems that summer is the best thing today,
And you definitely know it's cool!
Just lying about on the sunlit bay,
I hope these holidays will never end
Back to school, as busy as a bee.
Write notes to all my friends
I was just in a dream, as you can see
Oh no! It's time to go to school!
I spent these holidays like a fool.

Sarah Browning (10)
St Peter's CE Primary School, Wirral

Christmas Eve

C hildren playing in the snow
H aving fun as they go,
R unning around, snowball fights,
I cy weather cold nights,
S anta's coming on his way,
T urkey's ready for Christmas day,
M um's been shopping,
A ll week long.
S pending her money.

E verything's gone!
V ery happy it's Christmas Eve
E veryone's smiling it's time to believe.

Rebecca Leeman (9)
St Peter's CE Primary School, Wirral

Fear

When I get scared
I go cold and stiff
I cuddle up in my bed
And I wish my fear would go away.

When I get scared
I shiver and clench my fist
I cuddle up to my teddy
And wish my fear would go away.

When I get scared
I bite my nails and suck my thumb
I cry a little
Then Mum comes up and comforts me.

Lucy Roberts (9)
St Peter's CE Primary School, Wirral

The Sea

The sea is booming, boiling,
Is deep.
Tumbling, crashing, roaring,
The sea is still and sparkling,
From the sun which is shining.
It is cold and smooth,
Choppy then still.
But when the wind comes
And makes it feel fierce
With the crashing, trashing sea,
Now nobody's here,
Not at the beach,
Deserted.

Elizabeth Williamson (9)
St Peter's CE Primary School, Wirral

The Magic Box
(Based on 'Magic Box' by Kit Wright)

I will put in the box . . .
The whiteness of Spain,
And the greenness of the Antarctic.

I will put in the box . . .
A new city and a tenth planet
A bright beautiful butterfly
And a pink pongy pig.

I will put in the box . . .
The taste of a spicy curry at night,
The shine of an evening star
And the kind words of an angel.

I will put in the box . . .
The excitement of a child on holiday
The sadness of a pet dying
And the happiness of a newborn child.

My box is decorated with chocolates
And sweets with ice cream for handles
Strawberry jelly lid and love in the corners
Its hinges are made from green jelly bears.

I shall scuba-dive in my box
In the most gorgeous sapphire sea,
Until the Caribbean sun dies down
Then washed down with golden sand.

Hannah Rowlands (11)
St Peter's CE Primary School, Wirral

Rocky The Rooster - Super Strutter

The rocking rooster strutted down the street,
He strutted his style to the hip hop beat.

I'm a rockin rooster, so form a line.
I will rap for you, and it'll be just fine.

I'm the best at the rooster rap,
So come to me, and you can wear my cap.

All the rest can slip on butter,
Shout rockin rooster, super strutter!

Rachel Cooke (10) & Bethany Da Forno (9)
St Peter's CE Primary School, Wirral

A Nature Poem

N is for nocturnal animals
A is for the adventures
T is for the trees
U is for the uniqueness
R is for the rabbits
E is for everything that is *nature.*

Lilley Orme (10)
St Peter's CE Primary School, Wirral

My Budgie

Cherry - Chirper
Fast - Flyer
Mirror - Mocker
Tweet - Talker
Cage - Climber
Floor - Flee-er.

Anthony Brear (11)
SS Peter & Paul RC Primary School

The Sims

The Sims are cool
They make you drool

You rule their lives
You can even make them jive.

You can make them eat
You can make them sleep.

They could be a movie star
But they won't get very far.

You need friends,
To get you round the bend.

They can even be a magician
But they spend most of their time in the kitchen!

Making potions or spells
Whether it's nice or evil, we'll never know!

We can do anything with our Sims,
Just remember not to throw the game in the bin.

Georgina Edwards (11)
SS Peter & Paul RC Primary School

My Dog Shadow

Enormous - player
Speedy - runner
Spit - dripper
Food - catcher
Nippy - eater
Tap - dancer
Real - stinker
Long - leaper
Sorrowful - sleeper.

Alex Howard (11)
SS Peter & Paul RC Primary School

The Homework Machine

When your teacher asks . . .
Where's your homework?
You'll say, 'Here's my homework'

The next day,
In the middle of May
You get your . . . *score - 0!*

Put in a dime
And in no time
Out pops your homework.

You rush back home
You see your dog chewing a bone
You rush upstairs and . . .

You give it a test
It's just a pest
So . . .

6+6=66
3+3=33
What in the . . . ?

Put in a dime
And in no time
Out pops your homework!

Nicole Haviland (11)
SS Peter & Paul RC Primary School

Sadness

I am a tear falling on a coffin
I am a raindrop spitting on the gravestone
I am the ashes of the loved ones burnt to a crisp
I am a plant drooping and dying
I am a heart broken in two,
I am a star sucked into a black hole.

Sarah Hoyle (10)
SS Peter & Paul RC Primary School

My PC

I just can't get off my PC
I'm as addicted as anyone can be!
If I play anymore,
I may fall to the floor.

What game should I play?
Can I make disks out of clay?
My eyes can't blink,
And my brain can't think.

What does this error say?
Now I cannot play
My PC has broke,
I will ring the computer bloke.

The man has fixed my PC
And I'm as happy as can be!
Now I can play all I want,
And mess with the PC font!

Thomas Moscrip (10)
SS Peter & Paul RC Primary School

The Simpsons

They make me laugh
They are so daft,
I watch them all the time,
Homer is lazy,
He is so crazy,
Marge's head is full of hair
But Homer's is just bare
Bart is naughty
Lisa is brainy
That's the family
Very mad
Wouldn't you agree?

Tom McHugh (11)
SS Peter & Paul RC Primary School

My Sister Sam!

Samantha is my sister
So cute and cuddly
When she gets in a bad mood
She needs a bubbly.

Wah, wah, wah
She screams
She really likes her food
I hope she likes ice cream.

Samantha is my sister
So cute and cuddly
Hope next time you see her
She doesn't need a bubbly.

Kathryn Poyning (10)
SS Peter & Paul RC Primary School

Mates!

My best mates are Ness and Soph
Equally I love them both!
They're there for me through thick and thin,
They soothe my feelings deep within
We love to dance - it's really cool,
Sometimes we go for a swim in the pool
We might go to watch a movie
Maybe 'Honey' - it's really groovy.
That was just a little taste
About my two closest mates
But by reading those few words,
I hope you think they're two top *birds!*

Alex Sawyer (11)
SS Peter & Paul RC Primary School

I Know A Man

Whose name is Ray
Who takes me out on sunny days
To lovely places were we play
We play with cards - I win - hooray
I know he lets me win . . . okay.

Liverpool and Albert Docks on Saturday
Watch the planes land and fly away
We really have a wonderful day.

Mmm, egg and cheese sandwiches for our lunch,
Munch, munch, munch
We really are a happy bunch.

Good old Ray died last May
I'm sorry now he's gone away.
I love you Grandad!

Ashley Breckell (10)
SS Peter & Paul RC Primary School

The Monsters

The wolf man is growling
The mummy is waiting
The vampire is sharpening his teeth.

Frankenstein is charging
Can't bear to be waiting
Bogeyman stops him, hoorah!

Now all are running
No need to be waiting
But now they are coming
For you.

Amy Jones (10)
SS Peter & Paul RC Primary School

Sadness

I am the upsetting part of lying to people
I am the heartbreak feeling of truth about things
I am the roller coaster breaking down
I am a company closing down
I am the fish washed up ashore
I am a toy broken in half
I am some clothes thrown in the bin
I am a person run down by love
I am a tree as bare as bread
I am a book abandoned and old
I am a room, just empty and plain
I am the feeling of being left out
I am a person with nothing at all.

Charlotte Edwards (10)
SS Peter & Paul RC Primary School

Hawaii!
(Nonsense Poem)

Early in the morning
At 6pm,
I went to Hawaii
In Jerusalem!

The sun was shining,
As rain dripped from the sky,
A coconut jumped up,
And hit me in the eye!

I hated the sand,
So I went to the beach,
Then I had a yoghurt . . .
Life's a peach!

Katie Menear (11)
SS Peter & Paul RC Primary School

Baby Blues

Rattle shaker
Toy breaker
Hug stealer
Nappy carrier
Cake smudger
On going giggler
Sister kicker
Voice blocker
Little screamer
Big boomer.

Rebecca McGarry (10)
SS Peter & Paul RC Primary School

I Am An Animal!

There is a monkey inside me who is always there
                                            to help those in need.
There is a horse inside me who flies over every jump
There is a penguin inside me, who types at full speed,
There is a guard dog inside me, who roams the jungle,
There is a hyena inside me, which laughs at the wrong time
There is an elephant inside me who will make the
                                            sun come out on a rainy day!

Kate Burnett (11)
SS Peter & Paul RC Primary School

My Nan

My nan goes out on a Saturday night
My nan doesn't go out at all
My nan picks me up from school
My nan stays at home
My nan helps me with my homework
My nan does not help me at all.

Benedict Gillett (10)
SS Peter & Paul RC Primary School

What Am I?

Fast - runner
High - jumper
Mouse - eater
Food - pincher
Warm - cuddler
Door - scratcher
Fierce - guarder

What am I?

Hannah Heathcote (11)
SS Peter & Paul RC Primary School

Nans

Gentle - cares
Good - knitters
Big - huggers
Beach - groves
Slow - drivers
Bad - dancers
Pet - lovers
Funny - laughters.

Jazz Adams (11)
SS Peter & Paul RC Primary School

Happiness

I am the children on Christmas Day
I am Jesus born on that day
I am the trees growing new leaves
I am the sun glowing so bright
I am the person winning a game,
I am the children playing in the snow,
I am the fire warming someone up.

Rosie Cull (10)
SS Peter & Paul RC Primary School

10 Little Footy Players

10 little footy players went out to dine
One chopped her fingers off and then there were nine.

9 little footy players sitting by the gate
Swung it round and then there were eight.

8 little footy players on their way to Devon
One got snipered and then there were seven.

7 little footy players all licked a Twix
One was poisonous and then there were six.

6 little footy players went for a dive
One cracked his ribs and then there were five.

5 little footy players cleaning the floor
One got too dirty and then there were four

4 little footy players went out for tea
One ate too much and then there were three.

3 little footy players went to the zoo
One got eaten by a penguin and then there were two.

2 little footy players all met a swan
One fell in the lake and then there was one.

1 little footy player tried to eat a scone
Then he threw up and then there was none.

Josh Rylance (10)
SS Peter & Paul RC Primary School

Colour

I am the bluest ocean ever
I am the greenest leaf on the park grass
I am the golden instrument lying on the silver stage
I am the warm pink rose
I am the red heart being stuck on a card
I am the purple violet in the summer garden
I am the most colourful shell on the beach.

Maria Noone (9)
SS Peter & Paul RC Primary School

School Hallowe'en Disco

Frankenstein is dancing
Dracula is prancing
All night long.

Wolfman is howling
Mummy is growling
All night long.

The scary head is coming
All our hearts are drumming
All night long.

She finds out we are real
She turns into steel
All night long.

We dance
We howl
We prance
We growl
All night long.

Shay Donnelly (10)
SS Peter & Paul RC Primary School

My Limericks

There was a young man called Dale
Who wanted to eat a whole whale
He mashed it with cheese
And served it with peas
But couldn't quite manage the tail.

A boy from Westbury on Trym
Decided to go to the gym
He rowed and he rowed
He jogged and he swam
And now he is terribly thin.

Callum Hibbard (10)
SS Peter & Paul RC Primary School

Summer's Sun And Days

Blue sea crashing
The waves are bashing
The sun is beaming
Kids are screaming
The waters splashing
Surf boards are lashing
It's the end of the day
We'll set off and go away
The beach is quiet
And no one's here.

Lucinda Crosby (10)
SS Peter & Paul RC Primary School

My Mum, Your Mum

My mum is greater than your mum
Yes, my mum's greater than yours!
My mum helps me without me having to ask
My mum does that too.
My mum gives me lots of hugs and cuddles
My mum does that too.
My mum helps me with my homework
When I'm stuck my mum does that too
Maybe both our mums are great.

Daine Boden (10)
SS Peter & Paul RC Primary School

A Young Pet Squirrel

There was a boy from the Wirral
Who got as a pet, a young squirrel
It slept in a hat, along with a cat
Who was bald, had 3 legs and called Cyril.

Charles Nethercoat (9)
SS Peter & Paul RC Primary School

Happiness/Sadness

Happiness
I am the baby welcomed into God's family
I am the Christmas presents waiting patiently to be opened
I am God watching with love down on His people
I am the sun beaming in the daylight
I am the mother of Jesus when He was born,
I am the sea pushing the water onto the sand.

Sadness
I am the daughter of a dead man
I am the whisper of love broken
I am the tears of raindrops falling from the sky,
I am the happiness failing and turning into heartache,
I am the book torn into pieces,
I am the special teddy bear of love homeless.

Bethany Cumming (10)
SS Peter & Paul RC Primary School

My Stickers, Your Stickers

I have more stickers than you
I have 532
I have Gerrard and Edu
What about you?

Yes I have fewer stickers than you
But I have Owen and Cheyrou
I also have Hyypia and Diou
Which I think is better than you.

But I only need 23
For my Liverpools I only need Treore
So I am full of glee
And no one's better than me.

Do you want to do a swap?

Elliott McWilliam (10)
SS Peter & Paul RC Primary School

My Hamsters

I had three hamsters you know
Bubbles, Fudge and Hammy
I wish they didn't go!
Hammy hid in Grandad's shoe
A A A A Aaachoo!
Bubbles used to always play
I wish she could stay
Fudge liked to run in her ball
From living room to hall.

Darcey Moores (9)
Woodley Primary School

My Imaginary Friend

My imaginary friend is cool,
He never goes to school,
He stays out of trouble,
He's there on the double,
He's very handy but not for Andy,
My imaginary friend is sporty,
But he's sometimes snorty,
He's a dude but he can be rude.

Ellie Worsley (9)
Woodley Primary School

Football

Yellow is warning
Red you are off
You shoot you might score,
Football, football is my hobby
My goals are great.

Lewis Moore & Daniel Allen-Prince (9)
Woodley Primary School

Spider

Creepy, crawly
Hairy, scary,
Spider climbing the plughole,
Amazing adventurous creatures
Are not coming near *me!*
Scrubbing in the bath feel something moving on my foot,
Screaming *Mum*
Frightened and scared I am
Spider doesn't like the sound
Back down the plughole he goes!

Amy Redfearn (9)
Woodley Primary School

My Bed

My bed has moved away,
It didn't say goodbye,
My bed has gone to Daddy's house,
It has gone today!

My bed has gone on holiday,
And left his teddy bear
My bed has gone on holiday
Without anything to *wear!*

Ben McKinstry (9)
Woodley Primary School

Wildlife

Squirrels scattering by
If you are quiet you might hear a bird singing
A family of moles playing with each other
Hedgehogs rustling in the leaves
Foxes running around the trees
Fish swimming in a nearby pond
Plants growing over a toad's home.

Lydia Boswell (8)
Woodley Primary School

Puppies Are Cool

I love puppies,
I have got two puppies,
As soon as I come home from school I hug them loads
My puppies are cute, soft, warm, silly and lovely
They like you,
They are always warm when you hug them
My puppies are very ticklish
They jump up and lick you,
They are funny and intelligent
I really enjoy taking them for walks and runs on the field.

Joe Brennan (9)
Woodley Primary School

Colours

Blue makes me feel relaxed it also makes me think
                              of Manchester City.
Red makes me think of Manchester United it also
                           makes me feel scared.
Yellow makes me feel calm it also makes me think of stars.
Purple makes me think of lavender it also makes me feel happy
Green makes me feel excited it also makes me think of grass
Black makes me think of drainpipes it also makes me feel unhappy
Orange makes me feel strange it also makes me think of oranges.

Jessica Martin (9)
Woodley Primary School

Beds

Beds, beds, hot hairy high beds
Small beds, large beds, cosy beds,
Some warm, some bounce, some comfy
And some tall.

Toby Leigh (9)
Woodley Primary School

Just Another Day At School

Trudging along the muddy path,
It's another day at school,
I don't think I can manage,
Oh help what should I do?
I think we've got a test today,
I just can't remember
I'm going to get them all wrong,
I haven't even practiced,
Just another day at school.

Next day comes and it's a lot better,
No tests, no queasiness, no anything,
We had treats galore and prizes too,
I can't believe I really like school,
I'm going home now and I can't wait to tell Mum,
What a lovely day I had at school!

Natalie Davies (9)
Woodley Primary School

Me And My Outfit

Skirt is purple with a leather belt
With a silver buckle that looks like felt.
The T-shirt is pink with little thin straps
Pink looks stained but I don't mind.

Leah Brown (9)
Woodley Primary School

Dogs

D ogs are cuddly
O nly dogs are my best friends
G reat hours of fun with a dog
S pecial and clever.

Alesha Cresswell (9)
Woodley Primary School

School

Knocking on the door
Pencils on the floor.

In PE you learn new skills
Some people have to take pills.

Sometimes I forget my homework
And it makes me feel like a jerk.

When I have a good day at school
It's because I tried my best.

Rachael Thomas (9)
Woodley Primary School

My Cosy Bed

My bed is lovely
And really really long
It's so bouncy
Bouncy as can be
It's so cosy
And warm, warm, warm.

Ashley Dearden (9)
Woodley Primary School

Bouncing Trampoline

I bounce, bounce in the air
While my mum and dad stare,
It feels like my tummy's gone,
Far far up up
I daydream in the air,
At the birds I glare.

Rachael Millward (9)
Woodley Primary School

The Weasel

There was a dead weasel in my garden
When I went to dinner I asked to be pardoned.
I looked back at the dreaded creature
It shouldn't be near such sweet nature.
I wish I could go to sea and row ashore,
Wait a minute it's different than before.
Something's come in and ate its head.
I wish I were dead!
I think I'm about to scream
Oh thank goodness it was just a dream.

Sophie Drummond (9)
Woodley Primary School

Dogs

Dogs dogs,
Are loyal things
Dogs dogs
They chew your slippers
Dogs dogs
Are playful things
Dogs dogs
Are the best better than the rest!

Kimberley Robinson (9)
Woodley Primary School

Vikings

V icious they are
I n disgusting blood smells
K ings want to be more popular
I n the city they rule
N eed more jewellery how much more?
G uns not made but spears are thrown,
S pears are thrown for popular death.

Lewis Curbishley (9)
Woodley Primary School

The Dragonfly

D ragonflies fly everywhere
R eaching for the sky
A bright wing flying around
G reen and bright flying through the sky
O n and on the dragonfly goes
N ever stopping flying around
F lying around in the sun
L etting its wings flap around
Y et again the dragonfly flies around and around.

Ben Annable (7)
Woodley Primary School

SATs

SATs, SATs, I hate SATs
I say they're hard and my dad says I'm mard
They're not very nice
I'd rather eat a bowl of mice
When it's confusing I'd rather be cruising
SATs, SATs, oh I hate SATs.

Rebecca Cashin (8)
Woodley Primary School

The Ant

Down, down under the ground
Sleeps the tiny ant
With cold black skin and six tiny legs
It snores all day long
It starts to move to gather food in its back
Travelling through the grass collecting more food.

Jake McCormack (8)
Woodley Primary School

Beautiful Butterfly

Beautiful butterfly flapping its wings
Under the bridge it goes
It opens its wings and flies away
Enjoying the summer days
Raising its wings
Flying high, flying low
Little, little butterfly
Yellow as the sun.

Billy Gaskell (7)
Woodley Primary School

Gnat

The gnat hops to its prey
Then a sudden bite will do the trick
To air to ground
From the leaking rainforest
To biting the fly
Biting, biting everywhere
Who will be the next victim?

Nicholas Moorby (8)
Woodley Primary School

My Dogs

The dogs are happy
Crying in the house
The dogs are happy
Jumping up and down
The dogs are happy
When they jump at me.

Hannah Cooper (10)
Woodley Primary School

Ladybirds

L ittle ladybird crawling on the ground
A nd it's scurrying around a hill
D awn comes and it's crawling off to bed
Y awn it has woken up in time for a new adventure
B eyond and far away
I t's flying over a hill it's struggling very hard
R ushing away from me
D awn comes again and it's off to bed.

Megan Ormiston (7)
Woodley Primary School

Ladybird

L ying peacefully upon the ground
A lso listening to any sounds
D affodils you shelter under
Y awning every night
B arrels you hide in
I n the dark
R unning your best as can be
D eep holes you live in until you meet a she.

Michael Turner (8)
Woodley Primary School

Insects

I n the thundering clouds insects are all around
N ear ones you may hear but others you can't
S mall ones you never see
E ven if you can hear them
C rickets are very long and make a funny noise
T iny ones are really tiny and very small
S nails are very small and very slow too.

Olivia Wild (7)
Woodley Primary School

The Butterfly

B eautiful butterfly flying in the air
U p and down up and down it goes
T ill it gets sleepy and lands on a flower
T hen it goes in search of nectar
E xtremely hungry it is
R eally quickly it goes
F aster and faster it rushes
L ovely fine wings
Y ellow like a sunflower.

Thomas Hart (7)
Woodley Primary School

The Ladybird

L ittle ladybird scuttling about
A little leaf she climbs
D oing her best to reach the top
Y ou can't hear her as she tiptoes along
B eing kind and helpful to anyone who passes
I n a hurry she crawls back home to her stone
R eady to go out and have some fun
D ancing around in the daffodils.

Emily Stanyer (7)
Woodley Primary School

Spiders

S piders crawl along the ground
P assing the flowers
I like spiders spinning on their webs
D rinking the water from the river
E ating the flies caught on the web
R unning with their long legs.

Grace Wootton (8)
Woodley Primary School

Cats

Cats are wonderful
They eat with little teeth
Some cats scratch and some don't
Cats can be very smelly
They can be looked after well
Some cats are alley cats
Cats purr when they are happy
They have their own door called a cat flap.
Some don't have a home, because people don't look after them well
They just throw them out
Cats should be treated well, not be thrown out.
They can be ill-treated
Some cats miaow a lot at people
Cats are sometimes naughty
They can be really nice
Some are always happy.

Matthew Day (9)
Woodley Primary School

My Friend's Dog!

Scoop is cuddly, Scoop is cute,
But he is a rum-un when he chews my boot

He has white, soft, fluffy furr
All in a creamy whirl!

He has black beady eyes
As black as birds in the sky!

He is gorgeous I love him,
I wish he were mine, mine, mine

I would take him on walks every day I would never forget,
I would even take him on walks when it was wet!

Katie Fowler (9)
Woodley Primary School

My Bed

My bed is soft,
My bed is springy,
My bed is comfy
My bed is warm,
My bed is bouncy.

I am snoozing sleepily in my soft super bed
I wake up then I start snoozing again.

Jessica Barlow (9)
Woodley Primary School

Trampoline

I struggle to get on,
But the breeze pushes me on,
I bounce bounce in air,
Where shall I go?
On the roof top
Or stay in the air,
Or down below where my cat stares
When I'm up in the air,
I feel more relaxed
Than a bird having a nap.

Nicole Clarke (8)
Woodley Primary School

My Pet Cat

Everybody loves her
She really likes to purr
I think she's worth a lot of money
She is a little honey
She's a funny cunning cat
She'd probably chase a bat.

Rhianna Scott (8)
Woodley Primary School

Chocolate

Chocolate makes my taste buds tingle
It looks like it's ever so tender
It is nicer melted
Especially Dairy Milk
Nuts are not nice in chocolate
When you melt it they all crunch up!

Alyson Lees (9)
Woodley Primary School

On The Road

Driving in a car going down a road
Engines overheating, I don't know what to do
Lots of roadworks
Can't pull over
What should I do? What should I do?

Peter Harrop (9)
Woodley Primary School

Worms

W iggling through the mud
O ver and under they go
R eward for making the soil moist
M eet the people giant to them
S oftly they wiggle safely back home.

Kristina Rudge (8)
Woodley Primary School

Insects

Little insects are all around,
Climbing up and down like the grass
Colourful insects different colours like black, brown and green.

Robert Fox (9)
Woodley Primary School

Teacher Blues

I've got those teacher blues
I'm not ready for school
I feel so ill
I think I need a pill.
My head is like a drum
I really want my mum
Now I'm in my classroom
I want to leave soon
Get me out of this horrible place!
I'm in a disgrace
The children aren't kind
I'm losing my mind
Oh help help!
Now we're using felt
Glue is everywhere
Even in my hair.
In the playground there's a fight
It's a terrible sight.
I ache all over
I need a lucky clover.
I'm in a stress help me!
All the children can see.
I've sent Henry to the head teacher
Because he ate a horrible creature.
Jill's jumping on the flowerbed
Oh I need to rest my weary head.
Thankfully it's time to go home
Now I can't moan
It should be over now,
But I have a feeling it will happen again somehow!

Hannah Stevens (9)
Woodley Primary School